Matthew Willis

# Blackburn Shark



STRATUS

Published in Poland in 2020
by STRATUS s.j.
Po. Box 123,
27-600 Sandomierz 1, Poland
e-mail: office@mmpbooks.biz
as
MMPBooks,
e-mail: rogerw@mmpbooks.biz

http://www.mmpbooks.biz



**ISBN**
**978-83-65958-31-0**

*Editor in chief*
Roger Wallsgrove

*Editorial Team*
Bartłomiej Belcarz
Robert Pęczkowski
Artur Juszczak

*Text and research*
Matthew Willis

*Colour profiles*
*Chris Sandham-Bailey*

*Scale Plans*
Dariusz Karnas

*Proofreading*
Roger Wallsgrove

*DTP*
Stratus sp. j.

*Printed by*
Wydawnictwo
Diecezjalne i Drukarnia
w Sandomierzu
www.wds.pl

PRINTED IN POLAND

# Table of contents



# Acknowledgements

The author is indebted to the team at BAE Systems Heritage Brough for their assistance with the research and sourcing of the excellent photographs from their archive, without which it would not have been possible to produce this book. Heartfelt thanks are also due to Peter Menzies and David Weston for making available the log books and documents of A&AEE test-pilot Duncan Menzies, which threw valuable light on the test programme of the Shark and B-3 aircraft. Thanks also to illustrator Chris Sandham-Bailey, the team at MMP, and Tony O'Toole.

# Introduction

The Blackburn Shark is generally considered a minor chapter in the Fleet Air Arm's history. The contrast with the Fairey Swordfish, the Shark's near-contemporary which was developed for the exactly the same roles at almost the same time, could hardly be more marked. While the Swordfish is near-universally regarded as one of the most outstanding and justifiably long-lived naval aircraft of all time, the Shark served barely two years in operational squadrons and most of its career was devoted to unglamorous second-line roles. While the Swordfish became famed for many wartime exploits, the Shark faced the enemy only briefly, and without conspicuous success. The company that developed the Shark was even contracted to build Swordfish, and constructed many more examples of the Fairey design than its own. Yet the Shark actually had a slightly better performance than the Swordfish, handled just as well and possessed several more modern features. During their development it appeared that there was nothing to choose between the two aircraft, and in some areas the Shark had the edge. While much of the story of the Shark is a case of what might have been, the importance of the obscure service the aircraft did provide should not be understated.

# Background

In 1918, the Royal Navy made a major step in the field of naval aviation, with the creation of the Sopwith Cuckoo, the first operational torpedo aircraft intended specifically for use from aircraft carriers. At the end of the First World War, the Royal Navy had two aircraft carriers, HMS *Furious* and HMS *Vindictive*, which had been converted from warships with partial-length flying decks added. Two vessels to more advanced and complete designs with full-length flight decks were under construction as HMS *Eagle* and HMS *Argus*, again based on the hulls of partially completed ships.

After the war, a drastic reduction in naval air strength began, and HMS *Furious* was placed into reserve, while HMS *Vindictive* was turned back into a cruiser (albeit with a hangar retained for seaplanes). Of the Sopwith Cuckoos ordered, most wartime orders were cancelled. Nevertheless, the drastic scaling back did not fully curtail the new Fleet Air Arm (FAA), formed in the early 1920s as a semi-detached wing of the RAF, from developing the science of ship-launched torpedo attack.

The Blackburn Aeroplane and Motor Car Company was formed in 1909, and by the end of the First World War had considerable experience of naval aviation, not least in the sub-contracted construction of Cuckoos. The Cuckoo was a capable design compared with the preceding seaplanes, but could only carry the 1,086 lb Mk.IX torpedo rather than the 1,423lb Mk.VIII device which could potentially sink a capital ship. In 1917, the Admiralty drew up a specification for an aircraft that could carry the bigger torpedo. Blackburn submitted the Blackburd, while Short Bros. offered the Shirl. Neither aircraft was fully satisfactory, but the Shirl's performance was slightly better and, ironically, Blackburn was contracted to build 100 of its competitor's design. It would not be the last time Blackburn would have to swallow its pride in this way. In the event, the Shirl order was cancelled in 1919 and replaced with one for Cuckoos (which Blackburn again was contracted to build), but this created another opportunity for Blackburn when the Admiralty re-submitted its requirement for a torpedo aircraft.

In 1920, Blackburn developed the Swift, an aircraft that was a considerable advance on the ungainly Blackburd. The Swift was a large single-seater with voluminous fuselage of mixed steel-wood construction and broad-chord, two-bay wings. It was powered by a Napier Lion 12-cylinder 'broad arrow' engine of 450hp. Successful testing of the Swift prototype at Martlesham Heath led to a contract for further-developed aircraft, to be named Dart in FAA service, and later a production contract. The Dart entered service with the Fleet Air Arm in 1923 and remained in frontline use for a decade.

The Dart forged an almost unbreakable bond between the Fleet Air Arm's torpedo Flights (which had replaced the squadron as the standard unit of organisation in April 1923) and Blackburn. The Dart was replaced by the Ripon, a two-seat aircraft evolved from the Dart, and in turn by the Baffin, an updated Ripon powered by a Bristol Pegasus radial in place of the Napier Lion. In fact, Blackburn was the sole provider of torpedo aircraft to the Fleet Air Arm from 1923 to 1936. Blackburn's approach of evolving tried-and-tested designs, carefully introducing new technologies within a proven framework, stood the company in good stead and its designs steadily improved in performance and capability. In addition, Blackburn provided torpedo aircraft, of adapted existing designs or wholly new ones, to Greece, Spain, Japan and Finland.

One of Blackburn's carefully-introduced developments was the metal structure. Typically, British military aircraft were of wooden-framed construction in the early 1920s. The Blackburn Dart, along with the Fairey Flycatcher, introduced a metal 'core', with the forward fuselage, engine bearer and cabane built up from steel tube, while the wings and rear fuselage retained conventional wood framework. Metal structures were particularly suitable for naval aircraft because of the additional strength and, more importantly, their better tolerance to the marine environment. The Ripon Mk.IIC further introduced duralumin ribs and steel spars, and many Ripon Mk.IIs were rebuilt to this standard. The experimental Ripon Mk.III of 1928 introduced an all-metal structure for the first time, together with a more streamlined fuselage, and square-cut wings to simplify fabrication. The Ripon Mk.III did not go into production itself, but many of the features it introduced were incorporated into subsequent designs.

While Blackburn held a virtual monopoly on torpedo aircraft designs, aircraft for gunnery spotting and reconnaissance were a different matter. This was a hotly contested niche in the years immediately following the First World War, and no fewer than six designs were in service with the Royal Navy between 1919 and 1923, developed to a range of requirements with no consensus on the specifications such an aircraft should meet. Blackburn supplied its R.1 Blackburn design to the Fleet Air Arm as a response to specification 3/21, which required a fully enclosed cabin for the Observer and wireless telegraphy equipment; this aircraft had to compete directly with the Avro Bison, which was also ordered into production for squadron service. From the mid-1920s, the Blackburn and other designs began to be supplanted by Fairey's III series of biplanes, which came to dominate the spotter-reconnaissance role. In particular, the IIID and IIIF aircraft were the typical partners to Blackburn torpedo bombers aboard RN carriers, and served in frontline units until 1936.

By the mid-1920s, the pattern for RN carrier aircraft had fallen into three main types – the torpedo aircraft, the spotter-reconnaissance aircraft and the fighter. All three types could also carry bombs of varying sizes, but otherwise the roles were relatively distinct.

In 1930, officers of the new aircraft carrier HMS *Courageous* wrote a paper proposing a fundamental change to this orthodoxy. The paper promoted the idea of a smaller number of multi-purpose types for the Navy replacing the three accepted single-role types. The FAA's limited resources meant it could field only limited numbers of aircraft. Allowing each design to perform several roles meant that, in theory, the maximum could be extracted from each airframe, aircrew and square foot of deck and hanger space, making the whole air group a more flexible force. As a result, the Admiralty began to devote attention to which roles could be combined. The obvious solution was to combine the torpedo and spotter-reconnaissance requirements, as both were fulfilled by multi-place aircraft needing good endurance and load-carrying capacity. While the Fleet Air Arm had not had any use for two-seat fighters until this point, the Admiralty came to the view that a fighter able to carry a second crew member, who could navigate or operate a radio, could have a longer range than a single-seater. This would be useful for escorting strike aircraft, and would also enable the fighter to carry out reconnaissance in its own right. The appearance of the Hawker Demon fighter in 1931 seemed to confirm the effectiveness of the configuration. Therefore, the Fleet Air Arm's inventory began to evolve from highly specialised types into general-purpose ones.

At the same time, the view prevailed that carrier aircraft must necessarily have lower performance than land-based equivalents, because of the need to land and take-off in a much smaller space and have docile handling to allow deck landing. At the same time, it was assumed that carrier aircraft would not have to face land-based opposition, and therefore did not need performance that was competitive with land-based aircraft. Both of these assumptions were revealed early in the Second World War to be false, but in the 1930s were big drivers in naval specifications, in that they encouraged the Admiralty to demand characteristics that hampered the performance of naval aircraft.

# Development

The aircraft that emerged as the Shark had direct roots in the B-3, a prototype designed by Blackburn in response to Specification M.1/30, issued by the Air Ministry in March 1930. The specification replaced one that had been issued two years previously. It called for a torpedo bomber to replace the Ripon, which was itself only just entering service, while offering a significant advance in terms of load-carrying and performance – a 1,866 lb Type K torpedo or a 2,000 lb bomb with a total military load of 2,874 lb was specified, and a top speed of 130 knots (150 mph) with an endurance of seven hours at cruising speed. Considerable detail was set out regarding the stability and controllability that the machine must possess, including ailerons that produced a minimum of adverse yaw. Leading edge slots (either fixed or automatic slats, or an alternative mechanism) were required to ensure control and stability at or below the stalling speed. Any engine that had passed its 100-hour type test could be used, but the Air Ministry preferred either the Armstrong Siddeley Leopard or the Rolls-Royce H.10 (later named the Buzzard).

Blackburn offered the B-3, which showed clear lineage with the Ripon, but was somewhat larger and cleaner aerodynamically. The B-3, developed under Chief Designer Major F.A. Bumpus, incorporated a great deal of learning from the earlier 'technology demonstrator' Ripon Mk.III, including the all-metal structure, square-cut (single bay) wings and tail, and greater streamlining. The latter included a new radiator installation for Blackburn types, with two radiators enclosed in streamlined fairings beneath the

*The second, revised Blackburn B-3, the true forerunner to the Shark. The aircraft was powered by a Rolls-Royce Buzzard and incorporated innovations such as a monocoque fuselage with a 'wet' section containing the fuel. It is seen here in its 'Class B' test markings. (BAE Systems Brough Heritage)*

*Another view of the second B-3 in its initial markings. The large size of the aircraft is apparent from the figure standing by the nose. (Author's collection)*

wing roots. It was powered by a Rolls-Royce Buzzard IIIMS of 825hp. A single prototype was ordered later in 1930, with the serial S1640. In competition were designs from Handley Page and Vickers.

The Blackburn B-3 first flew in March 1932, and after manufacturer's trials was delivered to the Aeroplane and Armament Experimental Establishment at Martlesham Heath in August. No data on the performance of the first B-3 survives, and S1640 was lost in a crash in January 1933.

Blackburn was confident enough in the design to keep working on it, and built a second B-3 as a private venture. The new aircraft was far more than just a clone of S1640 though – it had an entirely new fuselage, of stressed-skin construction, which was very modern indeed by the standards of military aircraft in 1933. Moreover, the new B-3 featured a 'wet' forward fuselage formed of stainless steel, which contained the fuel without any need for separate tanks. The fuselage itself was completely watertight in order to help the aircraft remain afloat after ditching. The wing cellule was similar to that of the earlier B-3, but with the lower wings reduced in span, and full-span 'flaperons' on upper and lower wings. The second B-3 made its first flight at Brough in February 1933, and went to Martlesham for testing by the RAF in March. It received the serial K3591 in May. The new and old aircraft were both referred to as B-3 (which was indeed the 'Class B' registration of both machines) despite their considerable differences, but Blackburn applied the unofficial designation 'M.1/30A' to the newer version.

*The B-3 in its service markings as K3591, as it appeared at the Aeroplane and Armament Experimental Establishment, Martlesham Heath in May 1933. The aircraft was the best of the types submitted to Specification M.1/30 but did not receive a production order. (Author's collection)*

*Three images of the roll-out and first flight of the Blackburn B-6 on 24 August 1933, where it was flown by Chief Test Pilot A.M. Blake, with an uncowled engine and unpainted airframe. (BAE Systems Brough Heritage)*

*The B-6 now fitted with the short-chord NACA cowling exposing the exhaust collector ring. The prototype was the only Shark to be fitted with this style of cowling. The aircraft carries a dummy torpedo. (BAE Systems Brough Heritage)*

*The B-6 fully finished in its Class B markings with a Cerrux Grey finish to the fuselage and silver doped wings, essentially the same as production aircraft would receive. The Warren-truss wing strut bracing, which largely did away with the need for wires, is apparent. (BAE Systems Brough Heritage)*

The redesigned B-3 did not quite reach the performance required in the specification, though it was not far off. Its top speed was logged at 142 mph, and it could carry a military load of 2,735 lb. However, the other competitors to the requirement were experiencing difficulties too. The Handley Page HP46 was overweight and had many shortcomings, being considered unsafe for deck landing. The Vickers Type 207 did not fly until a month before the totally revised Blackburn B-3 did, but was initially promising, being 1,000 lb lighter than the Handley Page (797 lb lighter than the B-3) and capable of a top speed of 159 mph. During a test dive on 23 November 1933, however, the starboard wing failed and the Vickers broke up in the air.

None of the competitors was fully satisfactory, but the Air Ministry regarded the B-3 as having considerable technical merit, particularly its watertight fuselage[1]. By now, however, the Admiralty was fully committed to the idea of combining aircraft roles as described in the previous chapter. The Air Ministry

1 see p.145 K.J. Meekcoms and E.B. Morgan, *The British Aircraft Specifications File* Air Britain 1994

*Three images of the B-6 taking off from H.M.S.* Courageous *during the aircraft's carrier trials in 1934. It was still at this point fitted with the short-chord cowling. The short distance in which the aircraft carrying no offensive stores leaves the deck is apparent from the third image. (BAE Systems Brough Heritage)*

*The B-6 making a landing approach with arrester hook dropped – probably a practice approach given how high the aircraft is from the deck. The B-6 proved to have excellent deck-landing characteristics, and the trials led to a production order. (BAE Systems Brough Heritage)*

therefore combined the requirements of M.1/30 with another specification, S.9/30, which had been issued for a new spotter-reconnaissance aircraft.

This effectively created a new category of Torpedo-Spotter-Reconnaissance ('TSR') aircraft, and ended the procurement of pure torpedo-bombers for the Fleet Air Arm until 1945. Specification S.15/33 was raised in 1933, and appears to have retained most of the characteristics requested in both previous specifications, as the manufacturers who submitted designs offered relatively lightly modified versions of their previous designs, or improved versions that had been in train before the new specification was finalised.

The manufacturers still in the running included only one that had tendered for M.1/30, but two – Fairey and Gloster – that had prepared aircraft for S.9/30. This suggests that the Admiralty and Air Ministry were right to consider that the requirements could be met by a single aircraft, though it is somewhat surprising in retrospect that aircraft designed principally for reconnaissance could so easily be adapted to the considerable stresses and strains of torpedo carriage. That said, Fairey had already begun to develop a related multi-purpose torpedo/reconnaissance design for the Greek Navy, and this, being well advanced, first flew in March 1933. The Gloster F.S. (Fleet Spotter) 36 had not flown much before it was redesigned into the Rolls-Royce Kestrel-powered T.S.R. 38, which had higher lift wing sections to allow it to carry greater loads, and flotation gear, which the new specification insisted upon.

Blackburn already had a very promising design on its hands, but developed the M.1/30A further to S.15/33 in the shape of the B-6. The sealed fuselage section, forming the main fuel tank, was dispensed with, although the B-6's fuselage was otherwise similar to that of the B-3. The design of the wings was also largely carried over too, with a slight reduction in the span of the upper mainplane. In place of the conventional wire-braced cellule of the earlier aircraft, however, the B-6 introduced 'warren truss' strut-bracing, which almost completely eliminated the need for external wires. The wings were folded manually, but locked hydraulically with the aid of a system developed by Lockheed for Blackburn, where a hand pump provided the necessary hydraulic pressure. In addition, pneumatic wheel brakes were fitted.

Blackburn had up to that point been carrying out comparative engine tests with two Baffin prototypes, one fitted with an Armstrong Siddeley Tiger and the other with a Bristol Pegasus. Based on that experience the B-6 was designed to be fitted with either engine, but the prototype B-6 was powered

*The B-6 Shark prototype conducting torpedo dropping tests from Gosport in early 1934. As designed, the Shark's torpedo gear carried the projectile with a distinct nose-down trim, which the Fleet Air Arm requested be reduced. Nevertheless, the trials were successful. (BAE Systems Brough Heritage)*

by an Armstrong Siddeley Tiger. On paper, there was little to choose between the two engines. Both weighed in at exactly 1,180 lb dry. The Tiger IV produced more power than the contemporary Pegasus IIM, at 700 hp compared with the 635 hp of the Bristol engine. Furthermore, being a two-row, 14-cylinder engine, it had a slightly smaller diameter than the Pegasus which marginally improved the pilot's view ahead. However, there were numerous disadvantages to the Tiger, which Blackburn was becoming aware of as a result of its comparative testing, and which would later blight the career of the Shark. The allocation of the Tiger, at the insistence of the Air Ministry, is probably the single biggest contributory factor in sealing the aircraft's fate as an also-ran of aviation history. In 1933 the Air Ministry told Blackburn that there was no Bristol engine of sufficient power available (possibly as the Fairey TSR was lighter than the Blackburn, meaning it made more sense to fit it with the lower-powered Pegasus). The Shark was therefore committed to the Tiger for the foreseeable future.

The Armstrong Siddeley Tiger was a two-row 14 cylinder radial engine with a lineage that went back to the Jaguar of 1923 (and thus to the First World War RAF.8 design). It was moderately supercharged and drove the propeller via epicyclic reduction gear. The cylinders were made up of steel barrels with an aluminium alloy head, with two valves per cylinder. Supercharging was provided by a shrouded rotor located in the induction case behind the engine. Unfortunately, the Tiger was a lot closer to the end of a train of development than the beginning. From 1932, Armstrong Siddeley attempted to develop a new series of radical multi-row air-cooled engines, the so-called 'dog' designs, marking the changes from the existing engines named after cats. When this avenue failed, it left Armstrong Siddeley with no replacements for the existing range of engines, which were based on somewhat dated technology. The Tiger was arguably one attempt to stretch a design philosophy too far, by adding supercharging to the basic Jaguar-Leopard-Panther architecture and suffered from a lack of attention to its development while Armstrong Siddeley pursued its ultimately abortive radical designs. The Tiger would be plagued by reliability woes for its entire life, and would never realise the 1,000 hp its designers had hoped for – even the two-speed supercharged Tiger VIII never got beyond 907 hp. Meanwhile, in time, versions of the Pegasus were developed to produce 1,010hp.

Later, Major Bumpus would write that the company had made "*every effort with the Air Ministry to be allowed to produce a machine with the Pegasus III engine, with a view to switching over as soon as possi-*

*The Shark prototype after having been taken on charge by the Air Ministry and given Fleet Air Arm markings and the serial K4295. (BAE Systems Brough Heritage)*

*ble, chiefly because of the troubles that constantly recurred on the Tiger. We were always, however, met with the assurance that the Tiger was a perfectly good engine, and that, in any case, there were several hundred on order and they would have to go into the Sharks."*[2].

Meanwhile, the Fairey T.S.R. – powered by a Pegasus IIM – crashed in September 1933 as a result of an irrecoverable flat spin, seemingly doing great harm to Fairey's chances of winning an order, even though the performance of the aircraft in trials had previously been promising. The stage seemed set for the Blackburn B-6 to take the lead.

The first true Shark – at the time still known as the B-6 – was constructed at Brough and first flew there on 24 August 1933, piloted by the company's Chief Test Pilot A.M. Blake. For the initial flight, the aircraft appeared with an unpainted fuselage (wearing only the Class B registration 'B-6') and fabric-covered flying surfaces in primer. The engine was initially uncowled, but soon gained a closely fitting NACA-type cowling that terminated just ahead of the exhaust collector ring. This must have been fitted quickly, as photographs show the aircraft wearing it before the airframe had been painted.

2 see p. 13 Carl Vincent, *Canada's Wings Vol. 1: The Blackburn Shark*, Ontario 1974

*Shark prototype K4295 fitted with float undercarriage ready to undergo manufacturer's testing on the Humber. The aircraft has now been fitted with a production-style long-chord cowling and Robertson oil-cooler, after which it was virtually at Mk.I standard. (BAE Systems Brough Heritage)*

*K4295 running up its engine on the Brough slipway with dummy torpedo fitted. Note the nose-down trim of the torpedo carrier, which was reduced in angle after the first few production aircraft. (BAE Systems Brough Heritage)*

The prototype later received a finish similar to Fleet Air Arm markings, a glossy grey fuselage with black upper deck, and aluminium-doped flying surfaces. At this stage it still carried no military markings and only the Class B identification. Its overall dimensions were similar to the preceding Baffin, with a wingspan of 46 ft. and length (as a landplane) of 35 ft. 3 in. but it was rather heavier, with a maximum weight over 1,000 lb greater than the earlier aircraft, and appeared larger due to the tall undercarriage and general bulk of the design.

After manufacturer's trials were successfully completed in November 1933, the prototype went to the Aeroplane and Armament Experimental Establishment at Martlesham Heath, where it joined its forebear, the B-3 K3591, which was then still undergoing tests on its handling and performance.

Ominously, on 10 December, during one of the B-6's first flights at the Establishment, assessing climb and level speed, A.&A.E.E. test pilot Flight Lieutenant Duncan Menzies noted in his log book 'engine dud'. A week later, during an engine test, the engine was again described as 'dud'. Finally, a properly functioning engine was fitted and tested on 5 January 1934, and the test programme continued in January and February.

Early in 1934, the prototype left Martlesham for Gosport, from where it took part in deck-landing trials on HMS *Courageous*. Torpedo carriage and dropping trials were also conducted during this period. These tests were completed successfully, and the machine was finally taken on charge by the Admiralty's Directorate of Technical Development, and the Air Ministry issued it with the serial K4295. More importantly for Blackburn, the Admiralty also placed a small order, for 16 production-standard aircraft, which Blackburn dubbed the T.9 under its old internal designation system, and B-6 under its new system.[3]

The B-6 returned to Martlesham and an air test was conducted on 1 May. In June 1934, all three prototype TSR designs were at Martlesham, including the redesigned Fairey machine, now known as the TSR II. In October, the name 'Shark' was allocated, in accordance with the new naming policy in which TSR aircraft were given the names of predatory fish, while fighters were generally given the names of sea birds.

On 1 December 1934, Duncan Menzies, flew to Brough to collect the prototype Shark, K4295, and deliver it to Martlesham for testing after its modification to near production standard. The following records the flight back in Duncan's own words:

*"I was flying down wind at 600 feet in bad visibility with a Wapiti in formation on the starboard side when the engine cut. An immediate gliding turn to port brought into view the only field that was green. It looked to be an impossible proposition but there was no choice.*

*"I had to admit to myself that I was undershooting and damned myself for a fool, remembering the number of pupils I had told 'always take the far hedge when your speed has fallen off rather than undershoot and hit the near one'.*

3 Blackburn was then in the process of replacing its type-specific internal designations where the prefix donated the aircraft's role (e.g. T for torpedo aircraft, F for fighter) with a simple sequential numbering of all types, the so-called 'B-numbers'

Another view of K4295, now at Felixstowe for trials at the Marine Aircraft Experimental Establishment in the summer of 1935, again with a dummy torpedo fitted. The first floats tried needed some redesign to eliminate swinging in calm conditions, but afterwards handling on the water was good. (Author's collection)

*"To my growing amazement it began to look as though I would make it. The Shark was on a light loading and cleared a six-foot hedge hitting the ground within 20 yards.*

*"The aircraft had brakes but they were never used. The wheels sank in the soft ground of winter wheat which provided natural braking up to today's Maxaret standards and at the end of the run there was just sufficient room to walk between the airscrew and the far hedge.*

*"The aircraft subsequently continued its journey by road and investigation proved that before this flight the fuel filter had been dropped. Although it was unknown at the time, this introduced an airlock into the flow from a tank designed to self feed into the main collector tank.*

*"I take no credit for this approach and landing, it just happened. If I had had the extra height I prayed for I would have gone through the far hedge for a certainty."*

The Blackburn B-7, a de-navalised and modified Shark adapted to meet specification G.4/31 for a general purpose aircraft. The B-7 flew in November 1934 and went for trials at the A&AEE in May 1935. (BAE Systems Brough Heritage)

It seemed to be a one-off difficulty that had caused the engine to cut out, though this would be just one of many failures relating to the Shark's powerplant while the aircraft was at Martlesham. Nevertheless, testing at Martlesham was promising. The trials programme showed the aircraft to be extraordinarily stable, in all axes for all speeds and loadings, engine on or off. The Shark stalled at 45 mph indicated airspeed, and during the stall, the aircraft behaved well, with no control snatching or any other vicious tendency. This was probably aided by the leading edge slats, while the flaps were found to be effective and to give good lateral control at the stall.

In fact, when loaded to the same weight as when carrying a torpedo and the centre of gravity at the forward limit, the Shark could not be persuaded to enter a spin. The test pilots considered that it might

*The sole Blackburn B-7 at the A&AEE Martlesham Heath in 1935, carrying a 250 lb General Purpose bomb on a carrier that, unlike those on the standard Shark, protrudes some distance ahead of the wing leading edge, presumably for C/G reasons. The B-7's naval heritage is apparent in the dinghy stowage compartment, for which the stencil is clearly visible on the rear fuselage. (Author's collection)*

be possible to spin a Shark with some difficulty, but noted that the aircraft would soon exit the spin by itself, and recovery could be achieved at any time by centring the controls.

The A.&A.E.E. test pilots noted that all the controls were free from friction and play, and were reasonably light and well harmonised for a large biplane, as well as quick in response at all speeds. The flap control was placed conveniently, easy and quick to operate, and effective. Although some change of trim was noted when the flaps were lowered, the aircraft becoming nose heavy, this was easily held on the elevators. The Shark was fitted with a variable-incidence tailplane, which could be adjusted to trim the aircraft for various conditions of flight, and this feature was used extensively during tests.

The wheel brakes, an innovation for naval aircraft of the time, worked well, being easy to operate, effective, smooth and progressive in action.

Extensive testing was carried out to assess the Shark's stability in a dive while heavily loaded – crucial when dive bombing or carrying out a torpedo attack. A series of dives were carried out at torpedo load (8,086 lb) and to give the C/G at forward and aft limits (6,340 lb and 6,860 lb respectively), from a height of around 9,500 ft, at various throttle settings.

Once again, the Shark proved to be steady under all circumstances. The controls answered normally at all speeds, with no instability or vibration, and no sign of 'flutter'. In every case, it was easy to recover from the dive. The only problem encountered during diving trials was one occasion where the emergency dinghy came adrift from its stowage in the rear fuselage, though it appears that neither aircraft nor crew came to any harm.

Landing and take-off were similarly straightforward, and no swing was experienced in either case. The undercarriage was described as 'very good', and the Dunlop wheel brakes 'efficient', which aided the Shark's already good ground handling characteristics.

The Shark's cockpit was found to be roomy, easy to enter and exit, and not unduly noisy, and the instruments were well placed and easy to read. However, despite the addition of a heating system (using hot air drawn from a 'cuff' around the engine exhaust) the cockpits were cold and draughty.

The Shark's maximum speed at reconnaissance load was found to be 150 mph at 5,000 ft, and its rate of climb at sea level was 860 ft./min at torpedo load and 1,100 ft./min at reconnaissance load. Absolute ceiling was 18,800 ft. at reconnaissance load, and service ceiling 17,500 ft. It could carry a military load of 2,721 lb

While the trials continued at Martlesham, the first small batch of Shark Mk.I aircraft was already equipping a front-line squadron. In December 1934, 820 Squadron gained its first Sharks, replacing the Fairey Seals it had operated previously. As it turned out, the squadron's early experience with the type resembled an extended test period rather than operational service (see next chapter). The Tiger IV engine was continuing to prove particularly troublesome, and 820 Squadron had to take on a flight of Baffins to meet its operational commitments.

Around this time, Blackburn produced an adaptation of the Shark design for an RAF requirement. Specification G.4/31 had been issued some years earlier for a general purpose aeroplane to replace the

*The B-7, showing the simplified non-folding wings to good effect. The B-7's upper mainplanes were also increased in chord slightly to increase the aircraft's load-carrying ability – the specification called for a military load of 1,653 lb. (BAE Systems Brough Heritage)*

Westland Wapiti and Fairey IIIF and Gordon. These machines were the mainstay of the RAF's 'colonial policing' work across the Empire, and their versatility and utility in hostile conditions were prized. The replacement would have to carry out a wide range of tasks, including light bombing, reconnaissance and army co-operation, and the RAF seemed determined to widen it further. In late 1931, the Air Ministry added coastal patrol, dive bombing and torpedo bombing to the requirements, to allow the new type to supplement or replace the RAF's Vickers Vildebeest bombers as well. The adapted Shark was known as the B-7. Differences from the Shark Mk.I chiefly concerned the wings. These were fixed, as folding was not required, and were of greater area in order to carry still greater loads; the increase was achieved by widening the chord of the upper mainplane,. The internal layout of the fuselage was also rearranged to incorporate the plethora of equipment required by the specification. It was powered by the same Armstrong Siddeley Tiger IV as initially fitted to production Shark Mk.Is.

The B-7 was finished in late 1934 and briefly trialled at Martlesham the following May. Unfortunately, while the ever-changing nature of Specification G.4/31 had initially rendered the Shark suitable,

*The first production Shark Mk.I, K4349, without its surface finishes applied. It was employed on engine trials and performance trials before going to 820 Squadron in November 1935. (BAE Systems Brough Heritage)*

*Another view of K4349 in its unfinished state at Brough, with a dummy torpedo fitted. This shows the nose-down trim of the early torpedo gear to good effect. (BAE Systems Brough Heritage)*

by 1935 the goalposts had moved again. The Air Ministry had dropped the dive bombing and torpedo bombing role some time before the B-7 flew, so by this time interest in it was purely academic. Cursory tests on handling and performance were carried out before the B-7 was returned to Blackburns where it was later scrapped.

The naval Shark, on the other hand, had impressed the Air Ministry sufficiently that it placed a full production order, raising Specification 13/35 in June 1935. This required Blackburn to produce three pre-production aircraft (K4880-K4882) and a further 53 production machines of the improved Mk.II variant, known by Blackburn as the T.9A. Six months after that, an order for a further 70 Mk.IIs was placed under the same specification.

The Mk.II incorporated a redesigned engine mount and various other improvements to strengthen the fuselage, wings and tail, that had been tested on K4295. In the meantime, a more powerful development of the Shark's engine, the Tiger VI rated at 760 hp, had become available, and this unit was specified for the new version – though one of the pre-production machines, K4882 was to be powered by an 840 hp Pegasus IX. Furthermore, the Mk.I aircraft then with the Fleet Air Arm were to have their Tiger IV engines replaced with Tiger VIs. The production order for Sharks was big enough that Blackburn could no longer build the Sharks from the ground up, and various elements were sub-contracted to other manufacturers. Boulton-Paul built Shark wing spars, for example.

The switch to the Tiger VI involved an unusual operation in the process to ensure the suitability of the engine type and its installation. The 100-hour test would normally be carried out by the service, but in this case, the Ministry asked Blackburns to assist, to help judge if manufacturers would be better placed to do this work than RAF squadrons.

Perhaps mindful of the perception that had been created by the Shark's unreliability in its early service, Blackburn sought to demonstrate very publicly how dependable the Mk.II with its Tiger VI could be. One hundred hours' flying was required to certify the combination, and Blackburn decided to attempt to carry this out within one week, sharing the flying among four pilots, Flight Lieutenant A.M. Blake, Blackburn's chief test pilot, and service pilots Flight Lieutenants G.M. Morris, H. Bailey and C.A. Ball. Given that the seven days provided only 68 'spare' hours in which to complete the 100 hour test, there was little margin for error, particularly given that a period of maintenance was scheduled after fifty hours' flying. At 3.45 am on 8 July 1935, Blake took off for the first flight. The trial period continued with flights of around three and a half hours duration taking place whenever possible between 4.00 a.m. and 10 p.m., with an average of around 35 minutes between flights, although it proved possible to turn the aircraft around in as little as 15 minutes. The exercise proceeded smoothly and it looked as though the 100 hours would be achieved easily. Unfortunately, on the sixth day bad weather held up flying, and at the end of the week, the team had successfully completed 98.5 hours flying. The additional 1.5 hours

*A section of Shark fuselage undergoing structural testing in the factory at Brough. (BAE Systems Brough Heritage)*

were flown on the eighth day. Even so, it was a significant achievement, and augured well for the Shark Mk.II's Fleet Air Arm service.

In the summer of 1935, the prototype K4295 was fitted as a floatplane, equipped with a trial set of Alclad floats. It was part of the specification that the Shark be readily convertible from land to water undercarriage, as it was anticipated that the aircraft would be operated from cruisers and battleships by catapult as well as from land and aircraft carriers.

The Shark's floats were described by the MAEE as having a 'very efficient' design in terms of the access to internal spaces, the shock absorbing strut attachments, and handling arrangements. The floats were divided into five watertight compartments, each provided with a large, watertight cover. One of these compartments doubled up as a stowage space, with a removable crate for storage of an anchor, drogue and other equipment, and the cover was consequently fitted with a handhold.

Each float was connected to the aircraft by three ball-jointed attachments (one at the front, two at the rear), designed to allow a small amount of vertical movement with rubber shock absorbing discs, which dissipated peak loading during landing or taxying in rough weather. Blackburn had designed the undercarriage so that each float was identical, without any 'handing', greatly aiding maintenance and replacement. As with the 'landplane', the floatplane undercarriage was split to allow carriage of a torpedo. The floats were fitted with hydraulic water rudders to aid steering when afloat. These hinged into the downward position for steering, and could be raised for recovery. The rudders would 'kick up' automatically if they struck an obstruction.

The testing of the floats on the prototype Shark, however, revealed that their handling on the water required improvement. Some of the attachments were too weak, and in calm conditions the aircraft swung badly during take-off and landing.

The floats were returned to Brough and modified, by reducing the depth of the keel in the forward part of the float. They were then fitted to the first production Mk.II, K5607, which was built as a floatplane and transferred to the Marine Aircraft Experimental Establishment at Felixstowe for further trials.

The performance of the floats was very much better with the modifications undertaken, and no further swinging was experienced. Furthermore, the MAEE test pilots found that the water rudders steered perfectly well in the 'up' position, and they were therefore locked in that position to simplify operation.

When rigged as a seaplane, the arrester hook was generally removed, and a handling rail to aid ground handling could be fitted to its forward attachment points.

Unfortunately, it soon became clear that the Tiger VI did not resolve all the problems that had been associated with the Tiger IV. The engine fitted to K5607 became unserviceable during the tests, and had to be replaced with a spare unit.

The Shark Mk.II floatplane was capable of 148 mph and its service ceiling was judged to be 11,430 ft. Take-off run was approximately 625 yards (30 seconds). Its stalling speed was 74 mph, and best landing speed was 83 mph.

*The prototype Blackburn Shark K4295 in the New Types park at the annual RAF Display at Hendon, 1934. The Shark, to the lower left, is seen in the company of new and experimental aircraft such as the prototype Fairey Hendon K1695, Saunders-Roe Cloud and Handley-Page Heyford, Boulton Paul Sidestrand J9178. (Author's collection)*

As with the landplane, the Shark floatplane handled very well. At all weights up to the extreme maximum of 9,300 lb, the controls were described as 'reasonably light and positive' and response was good. However, the automatic slots opened at too high a speed and acted unevenly, so in level flight at low speeds the aircraft tended to roll from side to side, which would require modification of the slats to correct. The adjustable tailplane was found to be effective for fine-tuning the aircraft's longitudinal trim at all C/G positions and with flaps up or down. As with the landplane, the Shark floatplane was stable in all axes and there were no apparent vices. The floatplane handled 'extremely well' on the water. Its turning circle to port was 70 yards and to starboard 60 yards, well within requirements. Control during take-off and just after alighting was described as 'distinctly good', regardless of C/G position.

Aside from a few slight, easily rectified problems, and the more serious matter of the engine's lack of reliability, the Shark had proved extremely satisfactory during testing. Unfortunately, the same was not true of the aircraft's early service.

*Aeroplane and Armament Experimental Establishment photograph of Shark Mk.II K8485, demonstrating the plan view very clearly, particularly the square-cut wings and the much smaller lower plane. (Author's collection)*

# Prewar Service

Thanks to the Shark's good early performance in trials and the Air Ministry's familiarity with the B-3, the Shark was able to enter service very speedily. As it turned out, this may not have good for the aircraft which seems to have picked up a poor reputation that it never really got over. In December 1934, after only the prototype had been fully tested, and concurrently with trials of production aircraft, the Shark Mk.I was allocated to 820 Naval Air Squadron, attached to HMS *Courageous*.

At this time, the RAF still had responsibility for naval aviation, and only when units of the Fleet Air Arm were at sea did they fall under full naval control, although around seventy per cent of pilots and all observers were Royal Navy personnel. The remaining 30 per cent of pilots and a proportion of maintenance personnel were RAF ranks posted to the FAA.

Despite the Shark's torpedo-bomber heritage, 820 Squadron had been a spotter-reconnaissance unit equipped with Fairey Seals. It was now expected to take on the full range of strike functions in addition to reconnaissance, at the same time as getting used to its new aircraft. (Front-line squadrons were also expected to assist with second-line roles such as towing targets for naval anti-aircraft gunners to practice on. The Shark could be fitted with a temporary wind-driven winch to turn it into an impromptu target-tug).

HMS *Courageous* sailed for the Mediterranean on 5 January 1935, and remained with the Mediterranean Fleet for nearly three months, though it appears that 820 Squadron took little part in fleet exercises because of the unreliability of its Tiger IV engines. At the end of March, the carrier returned to UK waters to take part in Exercise 'AB', which aimed '*to exercise submarines in locating, reporting and attacking a fleet; to exercise aircraft in locating, reporting and attacking a fleet; to exercise co-operation*

***This and opposite page top:*** *The fourth production Shark Mk.I, K4352, code 740. This aircraft was allocated to 820 Squadron in January 1935. It was detached to the Royal Aircraft Establishment the following month before being shipped to Aboukir in January 1936 when 820 Squadron was sent to the Eastern Mediterranean to protect the Suez Canal in the event of the Abyssinian crisis escalating. (BAE Systems Brough Heritage)*

*between aircraft and submarines; to exercise a fleet in resisting air attack*'.[1] As such, RAF flying boats, submarines and shore-based aircraft were involved with some naval units on the 'Blue' side facing the 'Red' naval forces, which included HMS *Courageous* and her half-sister HMS *Furious*.

HMS *Courageous* and her aircraft took a largely defensive role in the exercise, restricted to anti-submarine and airborne early warning patrols, the attacks on shore bases being carried out by aircraft from HMS *Furious* and the catapult-launched seaplanes of HMS *Valiant* and HMS *Nelson*. The squadron's low-key role ended when the squadron disembarked at Gosport at the end of the exercise.

The Sharks of HMS *Courageous* would, however, take a leading role in the Naval Review of July that year. There had not been a full Royal review of the Fleet since 1924, but the Silver Jubilee of King George V provided the Royal Navy with an opportunity to show how it had modernised in that period. As HMS *Glorious* was in refit, HMS *Hermes* on the China Station and HMS *Argus* in reserve, HMS *Courageous* would, with HMS *Furious*, be one of only two carriers taking a full part (*Glorious*' aircraft would be involved, having disembarked to Gosport).

When plans were first drawn up at the beginning of 1935,[2] the Fleet Air Arm was to play a major role in the Review for the first time – the preceding 1924 review had a mere three aircraft in flight, while

1 *Report on Exercise 'AB' – 25th March 1935*, within National Archives file ADM 116/3872

2 *Jubilee Naval Review July 1935 Fleet Air Arm Flypast Arrangements*, National Archives file ADM 106/3022

*Shark Mk.I K4330/647 of 820 Squadron over the Great Pyramid at Giza in 1936, during the squadron's spell based at Aboukir. The unit's fuselage codes changed from 738-750 to 645-659 in December 1935. The squadron was present at Aboukir mainly as a demonstration of Royal Navy strength during the Italian invasion of Abyssinia rather than for any operational purpose. The Shark Mk.Is were withdrawn abruptly and shipped home when structural weaknesses were discovered in their engine mounts. (Author's collection)*

*The first Shark Mk.II, K4880, at Brough. The Mk.II was externally virtually identical to the Mk.I but included numerous internal and structural improvements. K4880 did not see service with any Fleet Air Arm squadrons, instead seeing out its life in experimental use – first at the A&AEE and RAE for performance testing, then back to Blackburns in late 1936 for development work, and finally to H.M.S. Pegasus in 1938 for buoyancy trials. (Author's collection)*

*Another view of K4880, carrying a torpedo. Note how the axis of the torpedo is now much more in line with that of the aircraft than it had been on the prototype and early Mk.Is, to the extent that the nose of the projectile is only just below the oil cooler. (Author's collection)*

in 1935 there were to be over 100. Plans included a flypast of all available aircraft, a mock massed air attack on the fleet, and a demonstration of anti-aircraft firing against a mock high-level bombing and low-level torpedo attack (to be carried out with de Havilland Queen Bee pilotless aircraft).

The flypast of all aircraft over the Royal Yacht anchored off Spithead would take place in the early evening. At this time, 820 Squadron was the only Shark unit in service, and its aircraft were the newest in the Fleet Air Arm. The other torpedo and reconnaissance squadrons were equipped with a mix of Blackburn Baffins, Fairey IIIFs and Seals, which would all be replaced within two years.

The plans called for all the available Fleet Air Arm aircraft, comprising the air groups of HMS *Courageous*, *Furious* and *Glorious* together with shore-based aircraft and those from seaplane Flights, to assemble at Gosport on 14 July, two days before the Review. The flypast would take place in the early evening of 16 July, after which the aircraft would return to Gosport, then embark the following morning ready for the massed air attack at 11.30 a.m.

The programme for the Fleet Air Arm was undoubtedly ambitious and difficult to arrange. Various alternative schemes were proposed before it was decided that the massed air attack would be dropped, restricting 820 Squadron's role to taking part in the flypast. The Admiralty was nonetheless determined that the Review would emphasise the importance of Britain's naval air power.

The flypast comprised 114 *aircraft* – Flight magazine's correspondent noted "*in close formation, the machines, with Sir Alexander Ramsay, Rear Admiral Commanding Aircraft Carriers, flying in the lead, flew between the lines at an altitude of 1,500 ft and made a dive in salute to 500 ft when abreast of the Royal Yacht, the Victoria and Albert, anchored at the head of the lines.*" The correspondent further remarked that "*the formation and station-keeping were outstanding as they always are in the FAA, and the whole flypast was carried through in that efficient manner which we expect from the Senior Service.*"[3]

3 p. 76 *The King Reviews the Fleet Air Arm*, Flight, 18 July 1935

A formation of 820 Squadron's Shark Mk.IIs over Aboukir in February 1937, during aircraft carrier manoeuvres in the Eastern Mediterranean, ahead of the Spring combined exercises of the Home and Mediterranean Fleets. That year's exercises took on greater than usual importance due to tensions caused by the Spanish Civil War and unrest in Palestine. (Author's collection)

Since 820 squadron had disembarked after Exercise AB, it had mainly been based at Gosport, continuing to work up with its Sharks and trying to cure the various problems it suffered. Apart from a two-week spell at the Second Armament Training Camp (2ATC) at North Coates Fitties in April, the squadron remained at Gosport until the Jubilee Review. The Sharks' engine problems continued, however, and when the threat of Italy invading Abyssinia became acute in August, 'A' Flight was re-equipped with Baffins to enable it to embark on HMS *Courageous*. On 29 August, after a conference of Britain, France and Italy aimed at defusing the tensions had failed, 'A' Flight embarked and sailed for the Mediterranean, leaving 'B' Flight at Gosport to continue working up. (HMS *Courageous* sailed with the Home Fleet on its planned September cruise, but she, with certain other units, discreetly detached and sailed for Gibraltar – the move was made to avoid antagonising Italy by disguising the strengthening of forces in the area at least until they were sufficient to face the *Regia Marina* in combat).

Eugene E. Vielle, then an RAF officer posted to the FAA, described this period with 820 Squadron: "*I joined the half of the squadron that had been left behind at Gosport and began flying the Shark – a very easy aircraft to handle. Like the [Fairey] IIIF, it had a large open cockpit behind the pilot. The design of the wires and struts that held the biplane together caused it to make a whistling noise and it became known as the 'Whistling Shark'. As soon as the full complement of Sharks arrived, we expected to be sent by ship (with the aircraft in packing cases) to join* Courageous *either in Malta or Egypt.*" Instead though, the squadron continued training. "*We made perhaps one flight a day, working slowly through a training programme involving practice bombing, dropping dummy torpedoes, night flying and – on one trip to Farnborough – learning to be shot off a catapult ('accelerator') of the types used in carriers. These were originally intended for launching seaplanes off the port side at the front of the flight deck, but were used by us to leave more space for other aircraft to take off normally from the deck.*"[4]

Vielle here identifies a seemingly innocuous characteristic of the Shark that later caused considerable difficulties. The 'whistling' noise was only partly the result of the aircraft's unusual structure (which in any case had hardly any wires) – most of the sound emanated from the oil cooler. This had not been picked up during testing of the B-6 because it used a different oil cooler to the square Robertson-type

4 pp. 119-120 Eugene E. Vielle, *Almost a Boffin*, Dolman Scott, 2013

*Blackburn Shark Mk.I K4356/653 of 820 Squadron taking off from HMS* Courageous *in 1935-6. This squadron was the first front line unit to operate Sharks and the only one to operate the Mk.I. K4356 had a short career, joining 820 Squadron in February 1935, going with the squadron to Aboukir during the Abyssinia crisis in the summer of 1936, returning to the FAA pool in December and being struck off charge in March 1937. (Author's collection)*

production oil cooler, mounted between the front undercarriage legs. (It was relocated to the starboard lower wing root on some floatplane Sharks).

While 'A' Flight sailed for the Mediterranean, the remaining 820 Squadron Sharks were returned to Blackburn to have their Tiger IV engines replaced with Tiger VIs as fitted to the Mk.II, though the aircraft were not upgraded to full Mk.II specification.

The extent of the problems with 820 Squadron's Shark Mk.Is is possibly reflected in the gap of over a year before another frontline Shark squadron was formed. The second Shark unit (821 Squadron) did not receive its aircraft until March 1936, and was equipped from the start with the newer Mk.II variant. Indeed, there were so few Mk.Is available, barely enough to equip a squadron and conduct production trials, that they can be regarded as a pre-production version in all but name.

The Abyssinian crisis escalated once more in October with Italy's invasion of the African country. Neither France or Britain wanted war with Italy, neither were they ready for it, and their actions to resolve the crisis were only taken so far as to avoid provoking Mussolini to attack them. Despite Italy being in a poor strategic position to fight a naval war in the late 1930s, the Royal Navy was nervous about the possibility. It cannot have helped that the service's most modern and capable torpedo bombers were currently stuck in England having their troublesome engines upgraded.

In February 1936, 'A' Flight gave up its Baffins, and the remainder of the squadron prepared to travel to the Mediterranean with its Sharks. E.E. Vielle explained how the squadron was "*suddenly ordered urgently to go out to the Mediterranean to join HMS* Courageous. *We ferried the 12 Sharks up to Sealand, where they were to be dismantled and put in crates to be taken by ship to Egypt for re-assembly. The plan was that we would then fly them from there onto the carrier. We expected to be sent out in one of the many troopships on their regular runs to India and the Far East.*"[5]

Instead, the crew sailed on the liner SS *Orsova*, in some luxury and, having entered the Mediterranean, were surprised to see HMS *Courageous* returning to Gibraltar as they headed to Alexandria. In fact, it was not intended that 820 Squadron join her carrier, but to operate from a shore station, RAF Aboukir, to protect the Suez Canal from possible Italian attack, or to enforce sanctions if the League of Nations decided to impose them. It appears that no-one had told the squadron this!

According to E.E. Vielle: "*On arriving in Egypt, we found a complete shambles. There seemed to have been no planning on where we should go. We started by being stationed at Aboukir – a glorious spot on the coast, where we lived in luxury in the officers' mess and had nothing to do except swim, play tennis and other games to while away the time until our Sharks arrived in their large wooden crates. These crates, when emptied, were all we had to use as offices, as all the accommodation was already in use by the squadrons*

5 Ibid. p. 120 Eugene E. Vielle

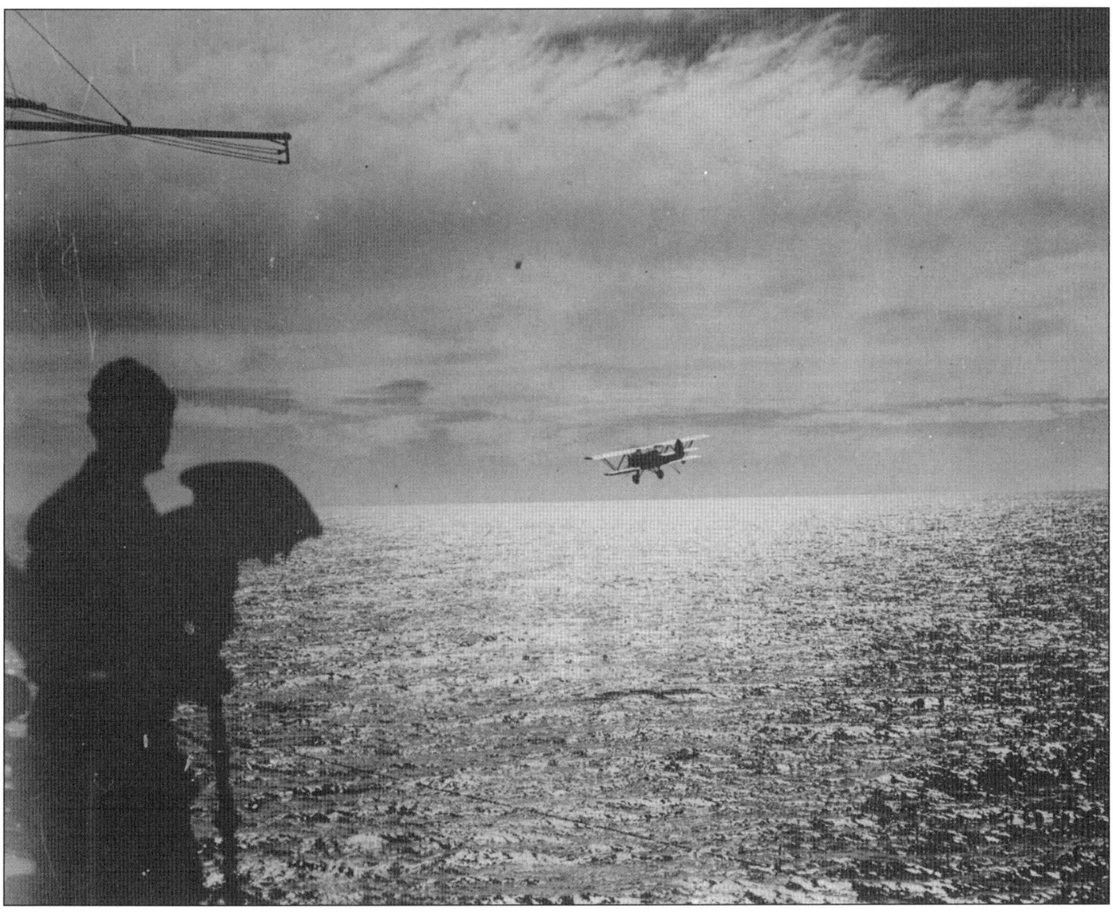

*A Shark takes off for an evening flight from H.M.S.* Courageous *during the February 1937 manoeuvres in the Eastern Mediterranean. (Author's collection)*

*A Blackburn Shark with its arrester hook lowered flies by the carrier HMS* Courageous *during Mediterranean Fleet exercises in February 1937. (Author's collection)*

*Shark Mk.IIs K8474/648, K8470/650, K8467/647 and K8454/658 of 820 Squadron, in a formation flypast of H.M.S.* Courageous *off Aboukir during the manoeuvres of three fleet carriers in early 1937. The other aircraft is a Blackburn Baffin of 810 Squadron. The fuselage band of all aircraft from* Courageous' *air group was blue. (Author's collection)*

*normally stationed there... The other half of the squadron had been left in Egypt to join us – making our total 12 officers, of whom half were Navy or Marine.*"[6]

He continues: "*Then, during the weeks ahead, and in very leisurely fashion, we carried on with our so-called 'training'. That included dummy deck-landings on a stretch of deck marked out as the deck of a carrier, or flying around aimlessly while our Observer played about with his Morse key, trying to contact various radio stations. On one occasion I was sent by lorry into the desert with a radio operator to set up a beacon there. One of the pilots spotted us and decided to 'buzz' us. He flew directly towards me at low level. It was one of the most terrifying moments of my life.*"[7]

The Squadron continued training, including deck-landing practice aboard HMS *Glorious*, before moving to Heliopolis at the other end of the Suez Canal in April. Here, a further serious problem with the Shark Mk.I was to manifest itself:

"*I was cruising at about three thousand feet near the airfield, with an observer in the rear cockpit, when I suddenly felt an extremely strong vibration. The controls acted normally and the vibration did not feel aerodynamic in nature. But the moment I altered the engine setting, the vibration changed. I sensed danger – and reacted immediately. I not only closed the throttle – but also switched off the engine. That almost certainly saved our lives.*

"*'Prepare for forced landing,' I shouted down the Gosport tube to Lieut. Wood, my observer, 'strap in tightly.'*

"*I surveyed the ground beneath us. Plenty of sand everywhere. No problem, and the airfield itself was not too far away. I had practised forced landings often, but usually with the engine ticking over. This time my propeller was stationary, causing extra drag and a steeper descent – but I managed to land just inside the airfield boundary.*

"*My aircraft was towed to the parking area, where Sergeant Pope listened carefully to my reasons for my actions resulting in the forced landing. He climbed up a stepladder and removed the cowling to examine the long metal struts that held the engine to the fuselage. Then one of the legs of the stepladder began sinking into the sand. He grabbed hold of one of the main struts securing the engine to the fuselage to steady himself, and it came clean off in his hand, causing him to fall and hurt his ankle. It was a scene I shall never forget – Sergeant Pope lying on the ground, holding the broken metal beam, staring up at the engine incredulously, and swearing at the pain in his leg. Two mechanics were also looking up at the engine in disbelief. Lieut. Wood was congratulating me and I was thanking my sixth sense (which has saved me many times since) for causing me to switch off the engine when I did. Had I not done so, the engine would have almost certainly torn free and fallen off – making the aircraft so uncontrollable that we would not have even been able to get out and use our parachutes.*

"*The remaining struts holding the engine were all found to be cracked and on the point of failure too. An urgent examination of our other Sharks revealed that most had serious cracks too. Our aircraft were obvious-*

6 Ibid. p. 121

7 Ibid. p. 122

*ly too dangerous to fly without major modifications to the engine mountings. They were dismantled and put back into their packing cases to be returned to Blackburns in England.*"[8]

With the Mk.I clearly unfit for operation, the 16 aircraft of that type were declared obsolete in early 1937. Most were struck off charge, several of these ending their days as catapult test dummies, while a few became instructional airframes. When 820 Squadron returned home it was re-equipped with Shark Mk.IIs.

Two more squadrons joined 820 operating Sharks in 1936, as well as a seaplane Flight providing catapult floatplanes for battleships. The squadrons were Nos. 821 and 822, receiving their Sharks in March and November 1936 respectively. The former was part of HMS *Courageous*' air group, while the latter was attached to HMS *Furious*. The first three frontline FAA Shark units had all been spotter-reconnaissance squadrons equipped with the Fairey Seal rather than torpedo bomber units equipped with the Blackburn Baffin (which were eventually replaced in all but one squadron with the Fairey Swordfish). The reasons for this are unclear, though it may be that familiarity with a given engine in the each squadron was a factor. The Seal was powered by a similar engine to that of the Shark produced by the same manufacturer (the Armstrong Siddeley Panther two-row 14-cylinder radial), while the Baffin and Fairey Swordfish were powered by variants of the Bristol Pegasus.

The seaplane Flight was No.444, a mixed unit, which took on some Sharks in addition to a variety of other types in March. (Its main equipment had been the Fairey IIIF, but in 1936 the Flight began to operate the Supermarine Seagull Mk.V/Walrus, Fairey Seal and Swordfish, as well as the Shark) This unit was based at Lee-on-Solent and provided catapult aircraft to some of the capital ships of the Home Fleet, namely the battleship HMS *Barham* and the battle cruisers HMS *Renown* and (from May 1936) HMS *Repulse*. The Flight was allocated four Sharks for operation from the *Repulse*, including K5623 coded '089' and K5624 coded '091'. (In addition, K5625 and K5626 were delivered to the Flight at RAF Mount Batten for *Repulse*, but no codes are known and it is not clear if they ever operated from the battle cruiser).

8 Ibid. pp.126-7

*A heavily edited composite photograph made up of at least three separate images, issued to the press during the Mediterranean Fleet Exercises in February 1937. The image shows HMS* Courageous, *with aircraft in flight that have clearly been superimposed, including '654' (probably K8468 of 820 Squadron). (Author's collection)*

*A mass take-off of Shark Mk.IIs from H.M.S.* Courageous *during the 1937 Coast Defence exercises. The lead aircraft is K5625/680 of 821 Squadron, which joined 821 aboard Courageous from 444 Catapult Flight in 1936. In May 1937, K5625 was damaged by crashing into the carrier's funnel, and returned home for repairs. The aircraft '528' towards the rear on the left is from 810 Squadron, which converted to Sharks in April 1937. (Author's collection)*

When the 400-series series Flights were replaced with 700-series units, part of 444 Flight became 705 Flight, equipped with two Swordfish and the two Sharks that had been attached to HMS *Repulse*.

In January 1937 the Air Ministry placed two orders for a further improved Shark, the Mk.III, of 45 aircraft (K8891-K8935) and 50 aircraft (L2337-L2386). Contrary to some sources, these were all powered by Tiger VI engines and not the Rolls-Royce Pegasus IIIM3, although the aircraft was designed to accept either engine. (Blackburn had wanted to use the Bristol engine, and built a demonstrator with that powerplant which received favourable reports from the A.&A.E.E., but the Air Ministry continued to insist on the Tiger). Some, though by no means all, were fitted with three-blade propellers (with metal hub and detachable compressed plywood blades). The biggest improvement was the addition of an enclosed canopy covering the crew. This had a fixed windscreen and central section, with sliding elements fore and aft allowing access to the two cockpits.

Also that month, 810, 820 and 821 Squadrons embarked on HMS *Courageous* and 822 on HMS *Furious* for the Spring Cruise and combined exercises for the Home and Mediterranean Fleets. This involved three fleet carriers (the previous two mentioned and *Glorious*) and a large proportion of the Fleet Air Arm. These exercises took on a more serious tone than many in the preceding years due to the tensions in several territories surrounding the Mediterranean, and indeed, because of the Abyssinia crisis, there had been no exercises the previous year. The Spanish Civil War was in its second year, and the combined fleet was ordered not to sail within 12 miles of the Spanish coast. The Arab revolt in Palestine caused further headaches for the Mediterranean Fleet, which had to detach ships to Haifa to support local forces, splitting the Fleet's attentions between each end of the sea. So important was the air element of the exercises that the three carriers proceeded to Malta weeks ahead of the rest of the Home Fleet to carry out their own exercises in the Eastern Mediterranean.

The combined fleets' focus was on trade protection, and the Merchant Navy was invited to take part as it had in 1935. The scenario played out in March was a convoy that one of the two fleets, 'Red' and 'Blue', would have to attack, and the other defend until it reached its destination. The Sharks' torpedo attack and bombing capabilities made them vital to both sides. The squadrons concentrated on night flying and torpedo attack, which was time well spent considering the successful night attacks carried out by the Fleet Air Arm during World War 2, not least at Taranto. Over 100 ships took part.

King George V had died six months after his Silver Jubilee Review. With the ensuing constitutional crisis surrounding Edward VIII and his eventual abdication in December 1936, the anticipated Spithead Review for the coronation of the next monarch did not take place until May 1937. This did not leave

*On 13 October 1936 Flying Officer Solbe of 820 Squadron drifted to starboard while landing K8466/659 aboard H.M.S.* Courageous *and crashed into the carrier's island. Fortunately both Solbe and his passenger escaped, but the aircraft was considered a complete write-off and was pushed over the side. (Author's collection)*

much time to prepare, but the preparations for the 1935 Review was put to good use and the plans for George VI's review were very similar to the earlier event.

In the intervening period, the expansion and modernisation of the Fleet Air Arm had added materially to the force. There would be four aircraft carriers in the anchored Fleet, HMS *Glorious* and HMS *Hermes* joining HMS *Furious* and HMS *Courageous*. Around 140 aircraft were to take part in the flypast, themselves a distinct advance on those taking part in the previous Review – the most numerous aircraft in the 1935 event were Blackburn Baffins, Fairey Seals and IIIFs, while the 1937 Review would see four squadrons each of Sharks – 820 Squadron having been joined by 810, 821 and 822 Squadrons – and new Fairey Swordfish, with most of the older types phased out. Deliveries of the newest Mk.III Shark had begun a month beforehand, with 821 Squadron the first to receive one (K8891) at Gosport on 8 April.

Unfortunately, during rehearsals for the flypast, a shocking fatality occurred. This was described by E.E. Vielle. "*We were flying over the Solent on quite a bumpy day, which made it difficult to keep accurately in position... I noticed that the aircraft flying on the extreme left of [821] squadron was having particular*

*Blurry but interesting image of Shark Mk.II code 537 from 810 Squadron, during the process of forming up into Wing order over Hampshire for the 1937 Coronation Fleet Review for King George VI. No.810 was the shortest-lived of all the operational Shark squadrons, operating the type for only five months. (Author's collection)*

*Two more images of 810 Squadron forming up over Hampshire ahead of the May 1937 Fleet Review, with another Shark squadron behind.. Over 140 aircraft, including all four frontline Shark squadrons, were involved in a mass flypast of the Royal Yacht, though flying activity was somewhat curtailed due to misty weather. The nearest aircraft is K8486/531 which only arrived at the squadron the previous month. (BAE Systems Brough Heritage)*

*difficulty in keeping position. One second he was too low, and in a few seconds he was too high in relation to his flight leader. He was also rather too close to him. Both aircraft had observers standing in the open cockpits behind the pilots.*

"*Suddenly, as that aircraft on the left was descending from being a few feet too high, I saw his wingtip hit the elevators on the tailplane of his flight leader's aircraft. That forced the elevators sharply down and put the flight leader's aircraft into a sudden dive. His observer had not anchored his harness to the floor and I saw him thrown out of the cockpit clear into the air – without a parachute. I still believe that I heard his screams as he began his fall to his death two thousand feet below.*"[9] Shark K5608 had collided with K5609, with the result that Telegraphist F.G. Baxter was thrown out to his death. The damaged Sharks landed safely with no further injury, but it was a sobering incident.

The Review itself was affected by poor weather, and mist and cloud made assembling the massive formation difficult. The aircraft were meant to fly past the Royal Yacht in squadron formation, diving to salute the Royal Yacht as in 1935, before moving into Wing formation and once again passing the warships. Because of the weather, the squadron formation and salute was dispensed with. The poor visibility hampered proceedings, but over a million people still turned out to see the Review, and the sight

9 Ibid. pp.149-50

*The combined Home and Mediterranean Fleets visible through the mist as 810 Squadron's Sharks fly overhead. The flypast was led by the Vice-Admiral Commanding Aircraft Carriers, Vice-Admiral N.F. Laurence C.B. D.S.O. in a Shark. (Author's collection)*

of the Fleet Air Arm was unquestionably impressive. The next time a full, public Fleet Review would take place was in 1953, by which time the Fleet Air Arm had changed beyond all recognition. The two Spithead Reviews of the 1930s mark both the high point of the pre-war, all-biplane Fleet Air Arm and the beginning of its formation into a wartime service.

The Reviews also 'bookended' the career of the Shark in frontline FAA service, with the former taking part as the first squadron had been newly equipped with the type, and the latter as it was months from retirement. The decision to withdraw the Shark from frontline use may have already been made when it appeared at the Review. Even with the improved Mk.II model equipping the four Squadrons and two Flights (and the Mk.III on its way), the number of accidents and failures had persisted. Several fatalities had occurred due to engines cutting out at dangerous times, such as on take-off. Efforts had been undertaken at the manufacturer, the A.&A.E.E. and the Royal Aircraft Establishment (R.A.E.) to

*Shark K5657/902 of 822 Squadron, with a formation of the squadron's aircraft over fleet warships, a battle cruiser and destroyer visible. This aircraft was lucky to survive flying into a sandstorm on 21 November 1936 while flying from Aboukir, and had to force land on a beach. (Author's collection)*

*Shark Mk.II K5621/690 of 821 Squadron on floats taking off from Gibraltar harbour in 1936. The aircraft served with that squadron from March 1936 to March 1937. It was modified at Dumbarton in February 1938 and the following year shipped out to Singapore to join No.4 Anti-Aircraft Co-operation Unit, the only British Shark unit to meet the enemy in combat. (Author's collection)*

identify the source of the problem, which was eventually traced to the Robertson oil cooler. This device had been suffering tubes fracturing from metal fatigue, leading to oil loss and engines seizing. It was initially considered that the failures might be aerodynamic in nature and related to the whistling sound that emanated from the unit, but these problems turned out to be separate. (It is possible that the vibration associated with the Tiger engine exacerbated the tendency of the oil-cooler pipes to break). While the R.A.E. suggested modifications to the oil coolers, the decision was taken to replace them with Marston coolers, which necessitated changing the entire oil system. Although this seemed to solve the problem, the Admiralty and Air Ministry had run out of patience. The work was to be carried out, but the Shark relegated to second-line use, even though deliveries of the improved Mk.III and a programme of improvement for all Mk.IIs – including structural and powerplant improvements, and full upgrade to Mk.III standard – were still underway.

*Shark Mk.II floatplane K5625, which was delivered to 444 Flight in May 1936, before going to 821 Squadron. No.444 Flight was based at Mount Batten, providing catapult floatplanes to capital ships of the Battle Cruiser squadron. It is seen here being lowered to the water from H.M.S. Courageous' hanger using Blackburn's patent slinging gear. (Author's collection)*

*A lineup of Sharks undergoing overhaul at General Aircraft in 1939. All Sharks underwent a comprehensive programme of structural and powerplant improvements estimated to be equivalent to 1,000 man-hours per aircraft, and this was still underway when the Fleet Air Arm withdrew the Shark from frontline service. Note the inner part of the NACA cowling on the nearest aircraft. (BAE Systems Brough Heritage)*

For the time being though, all four Shark TSR squadrons were still operating their aircraft and starting to show their potential. HMS *Furious* and HMS *Courageous* took part in the Coast Defence exercises in July, both using their Sharks to good effect as part of 'Blue' Force. On the Thursday of the exercise, HMS *Courageous* was detected early and subjected to a bombing raid from shore-based aircraft and a torpedo attack, but dodged the attempts to sink it to launch a concerted air attack on Portsmouth and Portland, as part of a combined assault made at Dawn. HMS *Furious*, meanwhile, sent her aircraft to bomb Plymouth, but a storm coming in from the Atlantic meant they had to be diverted to other targets. There was said to be "a touch of perfection" in "Blue's close-up attacks," caused by their forces "getting inside the defences' guard and catching them unprepared."[10] The Shark squadrons proved the possibility of successfully attacking a heavily defended port even after the carrier force had been discovered. One of HMS *Courageous*' Shark units, 810 Squadron, disembarked to Southampton to fly mock night bombing raids over Portsmouth, for the benefit of the Observer Corps and 'to lend an air of reality to the proceedings' without them having to undertake night deck landings.

In August, the last two squadrons still providing Sharks for catapult use on capital ships, 701 and 705, gave them up. That month, 822 Squadron exchanged its Sharks for Swordfish, and the month after that, September 1937, the other three TSR Shark squadrons followed suit.

There was still plenty of use for the Shark, however, especially with the programme of improvements, which ran to 1,000 hours per aircraft. As with the original manufacturing, Blackburn sub-contracted much of the work – for example, General Aircraft was given the work of reconditioning Shark wings. In January 1939, the company Secretary wrote to Blackburn complaining of the space taken up on the factory floor by the large mainplanes!

Even after the improvement programme, the Tiger engines were far from reliable. However, while leaking oil or shedding spark plugs would be of critical importance in operational service, in second line duties the impact tended to be less serious, not least as the engine could keep running under such circumstances. Some were converted to dedicated target tugs, receiving the semi-official designation Mk.IIITT.

There were a number of roles in which the Fleet Air Arm judged that the Shark could provide useful service. These included training Telegraphist Air Gunners in gunnery and wireless operation, Observers in navigation, and pilots in deck-landing and torpedo dropping. The Shark's robustness and docile

10 *Naval Review*, November 1937

*Blackburn Shark Mk.II K8483 'E' doing what it was designed to do, and never did in anger – dropping a torpedo. Here, K8483 is with the Torpedo Training Squadron, Gosport, releasing its 'fish' adjacent to a Royal Navy harbour launch from which drops were assessed. (Author's collection)*

handling made it suitable for these tasks, and many Sharks were delivered to the various Flights of the School of Naval Co-operation, which later became the 700-series squadrons of the Fleet Air Arm. Sharks were also allocated to training schools and Anti-Aircraft Co-operation Units (A.A.C.U.) for towing targets for gunnery training. Six second-line Fleet Air Arm squadrons operated the Shark when these units were formed in 1939, mainly in tandem with other types, before the outbreak of war in September 1939. No.767, a deck-landing training squadron operating in the Mediterranean from bases in France and HMS *Furious*, gave up its Sharks in July 1939, but the remaining five, all UK-based, continued to operate the type as war was declared. These were 750 and 753 Squadrons training Observers, and 755, 757 and 758 Squadrons training Telegraphist Air Gunners.

*Poor quality but interesting photograph showing two Blackburn Shark floatplanes flying over Plymouth in the mid-1930s. (Author's collection)*

*Evocative image of Shark Mk.II floatplane K8502, wearing the unusual code 'II', above the fleet in the late 1930s, including an Arethusa-class light cruiser, destroyer escorts and, in the distance, a Royal Sovereign-class battleship, which may be the Shark's parent ship. K8502 was delivered in 1937 and served with 820 Squadron before going to the Fleet Air Arm pool at Gosport. (Author's collection)*

*Factory-fresh Blackburn Shark Mk.III L2351, from the final production batch of Sharks. The first Mk.IIIs were delivered in April 1937, and were issued to all four frontline Shark squadrons, 810, 820, 821 and 822 as well as 701 (catapult) Squadron for HMS* Warspite. *The main external difference of the Mk.III was the enclosed canopy. This aircraft served at the School of Naval Co-operation from delivery in 1937, then to the Fleet Air Arm pool, before being converted to a target tug in 1938 for service at 2 AACU. (BAE Systems Brough Heritage)*

# Sharks Overseas

Blackburn designs had had moderate export success in the 1920s, in particular with sales of Velos torpedo-floatplanes (a two-seat development of the Dart) to Greece and the T.7B torpedo-bomber design for licence-building in Japan. Therefore when Portugal, Britain's oldest ally, issued a tender to the international aircraft industry in 1935 for a coastal defence and patrol floatplane for its naval air arm, it was natural that Blackburn would express interest. The Shark was a close fit for the requirement, and beat off stiff competition from manufacturers across Europe and the US in a deal said to be worth £50,000. Portugal ordered six aircraft, of which three were to be fitted out as bombers and three as long-range reconnaissance aircraft, though all could operate as bombers if required, as they were each fitted with three bomb carriers beneath each wing (four for bombs of up to 250 lb, and two for bombs of up to 500 lb). Although the three bombing aircraft were fitted with torpedo gear, this was not their

*Three of the six Shark Mk.IIA floatplanes ordered by the Portuguese Naval Air Service. The aircraft in the foreground is no.73, coded 1, the first to receive its certificate of airworthiness, on 22 February 1936. The aircraft behind is fitted with the long-range auxiliary belly fuel tank which was first used for an urgent diplomatic flight in 1937. The aircraft's finish was similar to the F.A.A. examples with grey anodised fuselage, black upper deck and silver-doped flying surfaces, but with the Cruz di Cristo in four locations on the wings and national stripes/crest on the rudder. (Author's collection)*

*Portuguese Shark Mk.IIA 74, code 2, taxiing in the Humber with a heavy bomb load. The Sharks were purchased as coast defence seaplanes and dive-bombers, and part of the reason Portugal decided on the Shark was because of the heavy offensive load it could carry. The load here is asymmetric, with three 250 lb bombs under the port wing, and a 500 lb and a smaller bomb under the starboard. (Author's collection)*

primary role (and indeed, no torpedoes were ever acquired for their use). The maximum all-up weight of the Portuguese Shark was 8,750 lb in the bombing role and 7,943 lb in the reconnaissance role.

The Portuguese Sharks were in most respects similar to the Fleet Air Arm's Mk.II floatplanes, being classed 'Mk.IIA' by the Air Ministry. Differences were minor, mainly being found in equipment such as instruments giving measurements in metric, and the installation of a Vickers Gas-Operated machine gun in the rear cockpit in place of the standard Lewis. The engine was a Tiger VIC, a slightly detuned Tiger VI. For the three reconnaissance machines, Blackburn developed a 160 gallon auxiliary belly fuel tank, resembling a bathtub, that fitted between the main undercarriage struts. This extended the aircraft's range from 690 miles to around 1,140. The six Sharks, bearing Portuguese '*Cruz de Cristo*' markings, carried out their acceptance tests for the Portuguese Naval Air Service, for which three Portuguese

*Two men in civilian clothing examining three bombs on port underwing rack of one of the Portuguese Blackburn Sharks, during the work-up and trials process at Brough. (Author's collection)*

*Blackburn Shark Mk.IIs of 6 (Torpedo Bomber) Squadron R.C.A.F. at Jericho Beach in the Spring of 1939. This unit was the first to be formed on Sharks in Canada, and it suffered many early difficulties from the Armstrong Siddeley Tiger engines this type was fitted with. (Author's collection)*

naval officers had been detached to Brough, in early 1936. Some Portuguese sources suggest that the Naval Air Service initially refused to accept the aircraft, though the British media was invited to view the trials taking place and speak to the officers, and no difficulties seem to have been reported.

The six aircraft were indeed accepted, and based at the Bom Sucesso Naval Aviation Centre, on the Tagus at Lisbon. They received the Portuguese serials 73-78, which were applied beneath the tailplanes, and code numbers 1-6 on the forward fuselage. One well-publicised use of the aircraft came when Portugal was accused of breaching its neutrality in the Spanish Civil War by refuelling Nationalist aircraft. Shark 74 (Code 2) was dispatched with a diplomatic courier bearing a document appealing the accusation for the attention of the Commission of Non-Intervention, based in London. The Shark made the flight from San Jacinto to Calshot over 22-23 October with only one stop, at Brest, making good use of the belly tank. The document was presented to the Portuguese embassy, and the Shark made the return flight from 28 to 30 October successfully, despite bad weather encountered on much of the journey. One

*The first Canadian Shark to fly, Mk.II 503, rigged as a floatplane, in front of a mountainous landscape. The photograph may have been taken with a reconnaissance camera, hence the background being in perfect focus and the aircraft being slightly blurred. (Author's collection)*

*Another photograph of 503, this time rigged as a landplane, against a gloomy sky. Shark 503 joined 6 (T.B.) Squadron in June 1939 and had a long flying career, later joining 4 (T.B.) Squadron and various second-line units before being broken up in 1944. Note the Light Series stores carrier beneath the port wing, carrying what might be flares or smoke floats. (Author's collection)*

of the Sharks was lost in a crash into the Tejo River in 1938, however, due to a catastrophic failure of the upper wing, and the remaining five aircraft were withdrawn later that year.

At the same time as the Portuguese Naval Air Service was issuing its requirement for a coast defence floatplane, the Royal Canadian Air Force was beginning its own search for such an aircraft. The RCAF was beginning a process of expansion and modernisation, and discussed its needs for a coastal patrol torpedo bomber with the British Air Ministry. The aircraft recommended was the Blackburn Shark, then just entering service with the Fleet Air Arm. Seven Shark Mk.IIs were ordered to equip 6 Squadron RCAF, with float and wheel undercarriage for each aircraft. They were issued the serials 501-507 and shipped to Canada, arriving from October 1936. The first four were assembled at No.1 Aircraft Depot, Ottawa, from where 501-503 were flown to Trenton, on Lake Ontario. The remaining aircraft, 504, was retained to enable the Depot to design and manufacture ski undercarriage and an enclosed canopy. The latter requirement was cancelled when Blackburn's designs for the Mk.III canopy were made available. The remaining aircraft were shipped straight to Trenton.

In June 1937 it was announced that Boeing Aircraft of Canada had been awarded a contract worth $132,000 to build 11 Shark Mk.IIs under licence from Blackburn. The order was quickly changed to Mk.III standard when the upgraded type appeared. The RCAF also agreed to buy two Mk.IIIs from Blackburn. Boeing hoped to be able to use one of these as a pattern aircraft, but in the event it was needed for squadron service. The chief difference in the Canadian Mk.III was the use of the 840 hp Bristol Pegasus IX, which both Blackburn and the RCAF had been pushing for from the start due to the ongoing problems with the Armstrong Siddeley Tiger. The Boeing-built aircraft were numbered 514-524 and 545-550, with the two Blackburn-built Mk.IIIs numbered 525-526.

It took some time to get the first Canadian Sharks properly into service, due to the now-familiar problems with the Tiger engine and oil system, exacerbated by the cold climate over-cooling the oil. When the improvement programme was developed by Blackburn, a set of kits was sent to Canada so the Sharks there could be brought up to the appropriate standard. Only when these improvements had been made, and the first Pegasus-engined examples arrived in April 1939, did flying really begin in earnest. Six Sharks from the squadron escorted King George VI during a sea passage from Vancouver to Victoria in May that year, following which torpedo training began at Jericho Beach, Vancouver.

*Sharks 507 and 503 of 6 (T.B.) Squadron over Vancouver Harbour in the Spring of 1939, at around the time the squadron provided an aerial escort to King George VI and Queen Elizabeth as they sailed to Vancouver. (Author's Collection)*

*One of two Shark Mk.IIIs built by Blackburn for the R.C.A.F., the first production Sharks to be powered by the Bristol Pegasus, seen here on the compass-swinging platform at Brough. The aircraft here was issued the serial 525 and the serial 508 applied in error, probably as the previous Canadian Shark had been 507. It was issued to 6 (Bomber Reconnaissance) Squadron in March 1940, but transferred to 4 (B.R.) Squadron the following month. (BAE Systems Brough Heritage)*

*The first Canadian Shark, 501, coded FG-O leaving the slipway at Prince Rupert, British Columbia, in 1942. The colour scheme has changed from the early one of grey, black and silver to an overall grey. Shark 501 served with three operational squadrons, 6, 4 and 7, this image showing the aircraft at the latter. (Author's collection)*

*Canadian Shark 506 loaded onto a boat for recovery back to 4 (B.R.) Squadron's base at Jericho Beach after force-landing in the sea. The Shark had been making a flight from Vancouver to the squadron's detachment at Ucluelet in May 1940, flown by Flying Officer J.K. Herriot (standing with hands in pockets) when it experienced engine trouble. Note the prominent Marston oil cooler beneath the engine's exhaust. (Author's collection)*

*Sharks of 6 (B.R.) Squadron R.C.A.F. at rest in the Spring of 1940. The aircraft now wear three-letter codes and red-blue roundels on the fuselage. The aircraft to the left is Pegasus-engined Mk.III 522 XE-K, while the tail of 524 (XE-M) is visible on the right. Canadian Sharks were fitted with slightly larger, more rounded rudders than their British counterparts, and the different shape can be seen fairly well in the case of 524. (Author's collection)*

*Flight Sergeant Hawkins poses in front of Shark Mk.III 545 FG-G of 7 (B.R.) Squadron in 1942. Note the armament of two 250 lb bombs. The Squadron was formed rapidly on Japan's entry into the war, and undertook daily armed anti-submarine patrols off the Pacific coast throughout 1942-43. (Author's collection)*

*Shark Mk.III 524 XE-M of 6 (B.R.) Squadron, loaded with 250 lb bombs beneath the wings and a 500 lb bomb beneath the fuselage. The larger, squarer rudders of the Boeing-built Mk.III Shark floats compared with those of the earlier, Blackburn-built floats, can be seen to advantage here. (Author's collection)*

***Above left:** A line-up of 6 (B.R.) Squadron's Shark Mk.IIIs in 1940. The short-chord cowling of the Pegasus engine compared with the longer Tiger cowling is particularly apparent in this image. The nearest aircraft is carrying a 500 lb bomb on the fuselage bomb-carrier. (Author's collection)*

***Above:** Two L.A.C.s of 4 (B.R.) Squadron, J. Smith and W. Thompson, pose with one of the Squadron's Sharks. The unit was based at Jericho Beach and Ucluelet between April 1940 and January 1942, when its Sharks were replaced. (Author's collection)*

***Left:** The wreck of 526 (one of the two Blackburn-built Mk.IIIs) being craned ashore at Prince Rupert after a landing accident in September 1942 while operating with 7 (B.R.) Squdron. The two floats, which became detached during the accident, can be seen, one at the pier on the right, and the other sticking out of the water beneath the aircraft. (Author's collection)*

# WW2 Service

At the outbreak of war, numerous second-line Fleet Air Arm squadrons and Anti-Aircraft Co-operation Units (A.A.C.U.) were using the Shark, and the RCAF continued with the type in its frontline strength, as a coastal patrol aircraft.

One use that Sharks were put to early in the war was the training of civilian pilots to naval standards, which was the responsibility of 780 Squadron, operating the type from October 1939 to November 1941. Another was torpedo training, with 785 Squadron at Crail under the command of Lieutenant-Commander P.G.O. Sydney Turner, where 13 Sharks fulfilled valuable service (and freed up operational types) until more service-representative aircraft were available in sufficient numbers. The Sharks were replaced by Fairey Albacores in August 1941.

Aircrew flying Sharks came to appreciate its steady behaviour and rugged construction. Former TAG Ken Sims wrote "*The old Shark was pretty docile and few people suffered qualms.*"[1] Squadron Leader D.H. Clarke flew the type with No.2 A.A.C.U. and later wrote that he considered the Shark to be "*the aircraft I would most like to crash in.*"[2] He recounts the story of a Shark that crashed into the sea (as a result of a pilot attempting to spin the undercarriage wheels by skimming the surface) and sank to the bottom, but was later recovered and put back into service "within the month".

Clarke described the typical use of an A.A.C.U. Shark: "*Our Sharks at Gosport were supposed to be non-operational and were used mostly for target towing – a D-type winch (with propeller-driven rewinding gear) being fitted on the port side of the rear cockpit. The drum of this which would carry up to 7,000 ft of wire and on the end of the wire we towed banners, sleeves, 17-foot wingspan gliders (which were launched off the centre-section like a miniature Mayo Composite) and sundry oddments.*"

From June 11-13 1940, No.2 A.A.C.U. provided aircraft to fly with lighted flares on target-towing cables over the Somme estuary, to help prevent E-boat attacks on the Dunkirk evacuations under cover

1 p.11, Ken Sims, *Telegraphist Air Gunner*, J&KH Publishing, 1999

2 p.32 Squadron Leader DH Clarke, *What Were They Like To Fly? Blackburn Shark*, RAF Flying Review Vol.XVII, No.7, April 1962

*Shark Mk.IIIs of 'C' Flight, School of Naval Co-operation (SoNC) at RNAS Ford in 1938. 'C' Flight was responsible for training Telegraphist Air Gunners (TAGs). Among the identifiable aircraft are L2365 and L2382, which were both late series Mk.IIIs delivered straight to training establishments after the Shark's withdrawal from frontline use. (Author's collection)*

*Shark Mk.III L2361 was delivered to 'D' Flight, School of Naval Co-operation at Lee-on-Solent in September 1937, the month that frontline Shark operation ended. After receiving modifications at Blackburn's Dumbarton factory, L2361 was issued to 'C' Flight S.o.N.C at Ford in October 1938 for training T.A.G.s, then 750 Squadron for Observer training, where it wore the code W1W – note the code in small characters on the fin. (Author's collection)*

*Shark Mk.III K8911 was initially issued to 701 Squadron as a catapult floatplane for the battleship* H.M.S. Malaya *before going to the Torpedo Training Unit at Gosport, then to 750 Squadron for Observer training. At this squadron, the aircraft was unusually applied with a red horizontal stripe, as seen here. It was fitted with the three-blade propeller with a metal hub and detachable wooden blades. (Author's collection)*

of darkness. Clarke flew a Shark on one such mission but had to turn back before reaching the patrol area of Abbeville.

The TAG training squadrons were also ordered to take steps to meet the enemy during this period, such was the pressure that UK air defences were under – and the need of the civilian population for reassurance. Ken Sims reported that at No.1 Air Gunners' School (755 and 757 Squadrons) at Worthy Down, "*about the time of Dunkirk all the aircraft were fitted with guns and took off and formated as a wing. We were impressed up there among it to see such a gaggle at one time but what we were supposed to be doing I never knew. I guess it was a show of strength to boost the morale of the population. Poor gullible souls. God help us if Jerry had appeared. Still, if our Swordfish were doing fighter patrols over the Dunkirk beaches, why shouldn't we protect England in a Shark?*"[3]

The largest second-line user of Sharks was 750 Squadron, which moved from Ford to Piarco Savannah on Trinidad in late 1940 to train Observers, in safety from German bombing. Around 40 Sharks were in use at one point, freeing valuable Swordfish for frontline roles. When the less-successful Albacore was withdrawn from frontline service, it was this type that replaced the Sharks in 750 Squadron in 1942.

---

3 p.12, Ken Sims, *Telegraphist Air Gunner*, J&KH Publishing, 1999

*Mk.III L2369 was another aircraft of the last production batch delivered straight to 'D' Flight SoNC (School of Naval Co-operation) at RNAS Ford, and later to join 750 Squadron for Observer training. The aircraft in the background, K5657, had a more eventful life, seeing service with 822 Squadron and surviving a forced landing at Aboukir after running into a sandstorm. It later went to the SoNC at Ford, then 757 Worthy Down and finally 755 Squadron for TAG (Telegraphist Air Gunner) training. (Author's collection)*

At least one Shark was used for experimental purposes in the early years of the war with the Royal Aircraft Establishment, when it began testing rocket projectiles as an aid to take-off for naval aircraft in 1941. The resulting Rocket Assisted Take-Off Gear (RATOG) was of considerable use in allowing greater take-off weight than would be possible with a free take-off. Where accelerators could not be used, wind over the deck was insufficient, or an 'overload' was required, RATOG could be used to help accelerate the aircraft to take-off speed. Shark Mk.II K5656[4], which had earlier served with 822 and 821 Squadrons, is known to have been used by the RAE in April 1941 during the early phase of testing. This included assessing the optimum number of rockets, the timing of firing them, interaction of the exhaust gases with the airframe, the effect of the failure of one or more rockets, and the safe jettisoning of the rocket carrier assembly. The Shark was suitable for this work because of the strength of its airframe and its general similarity to the Fairey Swordfish, which would be an important user of RATOG from escort carriers. K5656 was evidently returned to the Royal Navy after these tests as it is recorded crashing during a forced landing at Chilbolton while on the books of 755 Squadron on 22 November 1942.

Blackburn was informed by the Air Ministry in early 1942 that the Shark was considered obsolete for all purposes, and that all work on it was to cease with all remaining components scrapped. The last home-based Sharks were gradually phased out of service between 1941 and 1943.

In Canada, the last of the Boeing-built machines was delivered in early 1940. The RCAF planned two Shark squadrons to protect the Pacific coast and the sea-lanes along it from hostile shipping, but in the event, only one – 6 (Torpedo Bomber) Squadron – was formed. Two aircraft were retained for armament and development testing, at Trenton (502) and Ottawa (526) respectively.

At the outbreak of war with Germany in September 1939, the RCAF considered that the chief threat was likely to be submarines rather than the surface raiders the squadron had been formed to counter. As a result, the torpedo role was dropped and the squadron re-designated 6 (Bomber-Reconnaissance) Squadron. A detachment of two aircraft was established on the West of Vancouver Island while the remainder of the Squadron remained at Jericho Beach. The squadron was chiefly engaged early in the war in patrolling the coast and practising bombing and gunnery. A series of early crashes during take-off represented an inauspicious start to operations, but these were judged to have been the result of pilot inexperience and rough water, and once the crews became more familiar with their aircraft, no crashes were experienced for several years.

In April 1940, 6 Squadron moved to Alliford Bay in the Queen Charlotte Islands, while five of the Sharks were transferred to 4 (Bomber Reconnaissance) Squadron, which moved to Ucluelet in the

4 A photograph showing this aircraft undergoing RATOG tests can be found on p.109 of Geoffrey GJ Cooper, *Farnborough and the Fleet Air Arm: A History of the Naval Aircraft Department of the Royal Aircraft Establishment, Farnborough, Hampshire*, Midland 2008

*Two images of an unidentified Fleet Air Arm Shark Mk.III (with two-blade propeller) photographed with R.A.F. personnel following a forced landing in a field, probably just before its recovery. The R.A.F. provided the Fleet Air Arm with personnel for maintenance even into the early years of the war, as the Royal Navy had only taken full control of the service in 1937. The Shark, possibly K8490, which crashed into a hedge when force-landing in November 1938, appears to have suffered a failure of its port main undercarriage as it struck the hedge, and its propeller dug deep into the soft earth. It appears the machine was left overnight, due to covers being placed on the engine and cockpit. Note the bomb carriers beneath the wings. (Author's collection)*

west of Vancouver Island. The initial equipment was three Shark Mk.IIs and two Mk.IIIs, with some Supermarine Stranraers, but the Mk.IIs were soon replaced with more of the newer Sharks. The Mk.III 526, which had been fitted as a target tug, was allocated to 10 Squadron at Halifax to assist with gunnery training (though the squadron's regular equipment was made up of even more outdated aircraft, Westland Wapiti day bombers). Two Shark Mk.IIs, 501 and 503, were temporarily fitted with wheeled undercarriage and issued to 111 (Army Co-operation) Squadron in July 1940 to help that squadron train until its regular equipment of Westland Lysanders reached full strength.

One of 6 Squadron's machines, 517, was lost, with the death of its crew, in July 1940, in similar fashion to the Portuguese Shark destroyed two years earlier – the upper wing failed in a full-power dive. The squadron's other Sharks were inspected and found to have buckling of some wing ribs and movement in the mainspar. All 6 Squadron's aircraft were shipped to Vancouver for strengthening of the upper wing, but as a precaution they were not used as dive-bombers again. Naturally, this virtually curtailed 6 Squadron's activities for several months. Only one aircraft, 550, was available for some six weeks in early 1941, and the squadron was not back up to full strength until August, when it was able to continue its coastal patrols, which sometimes involved searching for missing ships and aircraft.

With the outbreak of war in the Pacific at the end of 1941, the Canadian Sharks of 6 Squadron RCAF were placed on readiness, and patrols were now fully armed with bombs. Only a few days later, however, the Sharks were replaced by Supermarine Stranraer flying boats, marking the end of the longest-serving frontline Shark squadron, which had operated the type for five years.

After the wing failure and crash of the 6 Squadron Shark, 4 Squadron carried out an inspection of its own aircraft, but this revealed no problems with the structure so patrols could continue with little delay. The Sharks were, however, withdrawn for routine overhaul in early 1941. After that, the routine of coastal patrols resumed. With the Japanese entry into the war, the squadron began armed anti-submarine patrols, but as with 6 Squadron, the Sharks were replaced with Stranraers within days of the Pacific war starting. The remaining Sharks were issued to the quickly-formed 7 (B.R.) Squadron at Prince Rupert, British Columbia.

In 1940, No.4 A.A.C.U. was set up at Seletar on Singapore with a Flight of six Sharks ('A' Flight) alongside 'B' Flight of de Havilland Queen Bee pilotless aircraft (and later 'C' Flight of six Swordfish). The unit was formed to help the island's anti-aircraft gunners practice, but it was to be a Shark from this unit that among the

*Three images of Shark Mk.II K8485 of a second-line naval squadron in flight over England in 1940, wearing standard Temperate Land Scheme camouflage. This Shark was ordered as a Mk.II in 1936 and served with various second-line training and target-towing units in the South of England in the early years of the war, including 758, Y Squadron Target Towing Unit, 780 Squadron and 774 Squadron. Both the R.A.F. and F.A.A. used the Shark until 1943 in various second-line roles such as aircrew training and target-towing. Despite being a land-based aircraft, K8485 still has its slinging gear and torpedo sight fitted. (Author's collection)*

*King George VI inspecting the Sharks of 753 Squadron at Lee-on-Solent in 1940 before its move to Arbroath in August that year. The squadron was responsible for training Telegraphist Air Gunners, and used a mix of Mk.IIIs and upgraded Mk.IIs. Identifiable aircraft are the Mk.IIIs W4P and W4G in the first row, and W4M and W4K (possibly L2376) behind. (Author's collection)*

very few to meet the enemy in action.[5] Before the outbreak of war in the Pacific, however, the A.A.C.U. was strictly non-operational. When fighter squadrons equipped with the Brewster Buffalo started to appear from May 1941, 4 A.A.C.U.'s Sharks were principally used on air-gunnery practice, though the aircraft's low speed left much to be desired considering the modern Japanese types that would be the Buffalos' adversaries in time of war. A short-lived experiment was the dropping of empty beer bottles to give anti-aircraft gunners something of the experience of being bombed! In the next few months, a number of 4 A.A.C.U.'s pilots would be transferred to operational squadrons. By October 1941, the Shark Flight had moved to Tengah.

Japan launched its attack on British territories on 8 December. Aircraft were in great shortage to British forces on Singapore, so a number of second-line aircraft were hastily pressed into service. The following day, two Sharks were among a number of aircraft sent on coastal anti-submarine patrols, one of which escorted a destroyer towing a broken-down submarine. The following day one of the Flight's Sharks on a dawn patrol was the first to sight HMAS *Vampire* and a minelayer returning from picking up survivors from HMS *Repulse* and HMS *Prince of Wales*, sunk in a heavy air assault, and escorted the vessels until relief arrived. Other roles for Sharks included searching for aircraft that had gone missing while defending the island against increasingly determined attacks. The Sharks, of which five were then serviceable, took on more of the A.A.C.U.'s work after some of its Swordfish were wrecked in an air raid on Tengah. Two of the Sharks were lightly damaged when Ki 43 fighters strafed Seletar on 15 January 1942, and two more were seriously damaged in a similar raid by A6Ms at Sembawang the following day.

As the situation became more desperate, more and more obsolescent and obsolete aircraft were thrown into the fray. Japanese forces on the Malay mainland were beginning to encircle the 45th Brigade, which called for assistance on 22 January. Two Fairey Albacores from 36 Squadron and a 4 A.A.C.U. Shark (K5621, flown by Sergeant Peter Ballard) were the only aircraft immediately available, so they were dispatched to bomb advancing Japanese troops on the road between Muar and Batu Pahat. K5621 (built as a Mk.II in 1936) was carrying four 250 lb bombs. A convoy of motor transports was discovered, 'nose to tail,' on the road, and the three aircraft dive-bombed and strafed the head of the column, doing "quite considerable damage" according to one of the pilots.

The Sharks were among the last aircraft left on the island, retained to help spot for the naval base's defensive guns. However, no operations of this nature were undertaken – with Japanese air superiority it would have been suicidal to attempt them – and the aircraft were probably destroyed on the ground.

---

5 For more detail on this unit, see Christopher Shores and Brian Cull with Yashuo Izawa *Bloody Shambles Volume 1: The drift to war and the fall of Singapore*, Grub Street 1992

*Fleet Air Arm ratings photographed at an airframes lecture in July 1943, using a Shark Mk.III with three-bladed propeller as an instructional airframe. The last Sharks to make a contribution to the war effort were static examples such as this and the Canadian examples used to practice carrier deck ranging. (Author's collection)*

The sole remaining operational Shark unit was now the Canadian 7 Squadron, which had a largely uneventful war but was no less active for that. In early 1942 the squadron's Sharks were chiefly employed on single-aircraft patrols lasting 3-4 hours, carried out several times a day. Activity increased when Japanese forces landed on the Aleutian islands in the summer of that year, and in October, WO2 Thomas sighted and attacked a submarine with depth charges. The submarine crash-dived, and it is not known if it sustained any damage. At this time, even Shark target tugs were armed and placed on readiness.

The accident rate among the 7 Squadron Sharks increased through 1942, due to the heavy workload on the now-ageing aircraft. In 1943, the unit began to receive Supermarine Stranraer and Consolidated Canso flying boats, and the last Shark operation took place in September 1943. Thereafter, all remaining Canadian Sharks were put in storage or converted to target tugs for service with 122 (Composite) Squadron. The Sharks in this unit, painted in all-over yellow with black stripes, were in high demand and were used heavily. As a consequence, and because of the dwindling supply of spares, the squadron's maintainers had an increasingly difficult job in keeping them running. The last target-towing sortie with a Shark was carried out in January 1944, and the last function performed by the type in WW2 was as deck-manoeuvring practice airframes on Canadian-manned escort carriers.

# Conclusion

The extensive tests on the Shark carried out by the A.&A.E.E. indicate that the aircraft was equal to the Swordfish in most respects, and even superior in some. Squadron Leader D.H. Clarke wrote "*in my opinion it was a far superior aircraft to the Swordfish. She could lift any load without effort and...was considerably more comfortable.*"

The A&A.E.E reports indicate that the Shark had equal or better handling, and its load-carrying ability was at least a match for the Swordfish's. Its performance was similar, and slightly superior in top speed. The Shark's factory-fitted enclosed cockpit made it more comfortable to fly, especially in bad weather. The Shark's drooping-aileron flap system was much more effective than that of the Swordfish.

On the other hand the Shark, if mishandled, could suffer upper wing failure (though only a few cases of this were ever experienced). The most serious drawbacks of the Shark were in its flawed oil system, which took time and trouble to fix, and its inferior engine, apart from the Pegasus-engined Canadian machines. Had circumstances been slightly different, there is no reason to suspect that the Shark could not have been as successful as the Swordfish. As it turned out, the aircraft still gave years of steady service which was great value to an expanding FAA and RCAF.

# Shark Colours

All Sharks leaving the Blackburn factory received a finish of 'Cerrux' grey (a pale, greenish grey) on the fuselage with a black upper deck, and aluminium-doped flying and control surfaces. Initially, red-white-blue roundels in 1:3:5 ratio and bright, pre-war colours were applied in six positions above the upper wings and beneath the lower wings, scaled to the differing chords of the mainplanes, and on the rear fuselage aft of the code. The aircraft serial in black characters was carried on the rear fuselage and repeated on the rudder.

In front line units in the pre-war period, Squadron/individual aircraft codes of three digits were applied in white on the rear fuselage within a forward-sloping band coloured according to the carrier air group the aircraft belonged to – blue in the case of HMS *Courageous* (810, 820 and 821 Squadrons) and red for HMS *Furious* (822 Squadron).

Portuguese Sharks had the same factory finish, but wore the Portuguese *Cruz de Cristo* markings on a white disc above the upper wings and beneath the lower wings. Their rudder was painted in vertically divided national colours of green-red, with the national crest on the dividing line. The serial was worn beneath the tailplane in serifed characters, and the code on the forward fuselage, just ahead of the forward cabane strut.

Second-line Fleet Air Arm Sharks in the pre-war period wore the factory finish, sometimes with unit codes (see below) on the fuselage side (e.g. 753 Squadron) or on the fin (e.g. 750 Squadron) but not in every case.

Canadian Sharks built by Blackburn wore the standard Fleet Air Arm finish, but wore the wing roundels on the upper and lower surface of the upper wing, with no roundel on the lower wing. Prior to WW2, the only individual markings carried were the serials, applied to the rudder in black characters. The Boeing-built aircraft wore a dull aluminium dope finish all over apart from a black fuselage upper deck.

In the Second World War, a few Fleet Air Arm Sharks seem to have had their markings modified to meet the 'Sea Scheme' (S1) (up to June 1940) with markings as per AMO A154/39 (April 1939), as at least one photograph exists showing a Shark of 758 Squadron with a blue-red roundel of 2:5 ratio on the fuselage. As the war progressed, Fleet Air Arm and RAF Sharks were generally painted in the Temperate Land Scheme, as befit all land-based aircraft – which all Sharks were by this time. It is probable that 4 A.A.C.U. Sharks were painted in this scheme, possibly with black undersides when night operations began. Considerable variations could be seen as aircraft were repainted at Squadron or Maintenance Unit level – for example, some Sharks of 753 Squadron had codes painted on the underside of the upper wing, while other aircraft had codes applied on the fuselage or not at all.

Canadian aircraft had their fuselage roundel changed to a blue-red device of 2:5 ratio from early 1940, and gained fuselage codes in the same period. Two of 7 (B.R.) Squadron's aircraft, 501 and 503, were painted in an all-over pale grey colour scheme from early 1942, with a yellow-blue-white-red fuselage roundel, and a blue-white-red fin flash covering the whole fin. Target tug aircraft were painted in an all-over scheme of yellow with diagonal black bands.

# Shark Data

Details given for Mk.II in landplane configuration unless otherwise stated.

- Length: 35 ft. 3 in.
- Span: 46 ft. 0 in. (folded 15 ft. 0 in.)
- Height: 12 ft. 1 in.
- Weights: Tare weight (torpedo load) 4,596 lb, (reconnaissance load) 4,596 lb; Flying weight (torpedo load) 8,250 lb, (reconnaissance load) 7,249 lb
- Total military load, torpedo weight – 2,721 lb
- Total military load, spotter/recon – 1,605.5 lb

## Performance

### Speed torpedo load

| Full throttle | | |
|---|---|---|
| | Top speed | Time to climb mins |
| Sea level | 137 | |
| 5,000ft | 149 | 6.2 |
| 10,000ft | 145 | 15.9 |
| 15,000ft | 127 | 43.0 |

### Speed reconnaissance load

| Full throttle | | |
|---|---|---|
| | Top speed | Time to climb mins |
| Sea level | 139 | |
| 5,000ft | 150 | 4.8 |
| 10,000ft | 149 | 11.7 |
| 15,000ft | 141 | 24.2 |

### Cruising speed/range

| Mph | Kts | RPM | Nautical miles | Land miles | Endurance hrs |
|---|---|---|---|---|---|
| Torpedo load | Height 7,300ft | | | | |
| 130 | 113 | 2150 | 460 | 398 | 3.5 |
| Reconnaissance load | Height 8,000ft | | | | |
| 130 | 113 | 2150 | 628 | 545 | 4.8 |

- Service ceiling – torpedo load 14,600 ft
- Service ceiling – reconnaissance load 17,500 ft
- Estimated absolute ceiling, torpedo load – 16,200 ft
- Estimated absolute ceiling, reconnaissance load – 18,800 ft
- Stalling speed – 45mph/39kt
- Maximum climb rate, torpedo load – 860 ft/min (at 1,000 ft)
- Maximum climb rate, reconnaissance load – 1,110 ft/min (at 1,000 ft)
- Powerplant: 1 Armstrong Siddeley Tiger VI, 760 h.p. (Mk.I, 1 Armstrong Siddeley Tiger IV, 700 h.p. or Tiger VI; Portuguese Mk.IIA, 1 Armstrong Siddeley Tiger VIC, 700 h.p.; Canadian Mk.III, 1 Bristol Pegasus IX, 850 h.p.)

# Units

## Front line Fleet Air Arm

- 444 Flight – Mar-Jul 1936 (Markings – Black side numbers 089 and 091)
- 701 (Catapult) Squadron – Feb-Aug 1937 (Markings – none)
- 705 (Catapult) Squadron – Jul 1936-Jul 1937 (Markings – Black side numbers 089 and 091)
- 810 (T.S.R.) Squadron (Markings – Codes 523–537)
- 820 (T.S.R.) Squadron (Markings – Codes 738–750 until Dec 1935, 645–659 Dec 1935-Sep 1937)
- 821 (T.S.R.) Squadron (Markings – Codes 678–691)
- 822 (T.S.R.) Squadron (Markings – Codes 901–914)
- Second line Fleet Air Arm
- 750 Squadron (Observers School) – May 1939-Jun 1942 (Markings – W1 and letter code, e.g. W1W)
- 753 Squadron (Observer's School – May 1939-Jun 1942 (Markings – W4 and letter code, e.g. W4G)
- 755 Squadron (TAG training/air gunnery school) – May 1939-Oct 1943 (Markings – X3 and letter code, e.g. X3L)
- 757 Squadron (TAG school/air gunnery school) – May-Aug 1939 (Markings – X6 and letter code, e.g. X6A)
- 758 Squadron (TAG school/air gunnery school) – Jul 1939-Sep 1940 (Markings – X5 and letter code, e.g. X5J)
- 767 Squadron (Deck landing training) – May-Jul 1939 (Markings – T4 and letter code, e.g. T4A)
- 774 Squadron (Armament training) – Nov 1939-Dec 1942 (Markings – O4 and letter code, e.g. O4F)
- 780 Squadron (conversion civilian pilots to naval standards) – Oct-1939 – Nov 1941 (Markings – individual letter code)
- 785 Squadron (torpedo school) – Nov 1940-Apr 1941 (Markings – individual letter code)

## Second line RAF

Little information exists on RAF Shark markings. It appears that 4 A.A.C.U. aircraft may have carried single code letters - K5621, which went briefly into action during the defence of Singapore, is reported to have worn the code R.

## Portuguese Naval Air Service

1936-38 (Markings – Codes 1-6 on forward fuselage)

## Royal Canadian Air Force

- 6 (Torpedo Bomber/Bomber Reconnaissance) Squadron – Nov 1936 – Feb 1942 (Markings – XE and letter code, e.g. XE-K)
- 4 (Bomber Reconnaissance) Squadron – Apr 1940 – Feb 1942 (Markings – FY and letter code, e.g. FY-E)
- 7 (Bomber Reconnaissance) Squadron – Dec 1941 – Sep 1943 (Markings – LT and letter code to May 1942, FG and letter code to Oct 1942)
- 11 (Army Co-operation) Squadron – Jul 1940 – Aug 1941 (Markings – TM and letter code, e.g. TM-F)
- 122 (Composite) Squadron – Dec 1941 – Feb 1944 (Markings – AG and letter code, e.g. AG-D)

*The structure of the Shark's tail, before being fitted to the rear fuselage and skinned. Note the flat underside panel. (BAE Systems Brough Heritage)*

*The monocoque mid-fuselage under construction at Brough. The Shark was the first monocoque aircraft that Blackburn produced, and it was built very strongly. (BAE Systems Brough Heritage)*

*Shark forward fuselage section on the structural testing rig at Brough showing the skinning to good effect. The cut-out in the top deck will be the trough for the forward-facing Vickers machine gun. (BAE Systems Brough Heritage)*

K
4354
S
1266
S
1358
K
4356

**Opposite page above:** *Shark fuselages nearing completion at Brough in 1935. This is the initial batch of Mk.I airframes – of those with visible serials, K4354 was the sixth production Shark and K4356 the eighth. Note the sealant applied to the panel joins to help render the monocoque fuselage watertight. The aircraft to the right rear are Baffins, the Shark's predecessors which were still being delivered as the first Sharks arrived. (BAE Systems Brough Heritage)*
**Opposite page below:** *Shark Mk.I forward fuselage showing the firewall, and tubular engine mount. This proved to be susceptible to metal fatigue and several failures occurred. It was improved on the Mk.II. The trapezoidal hatch just behind the firewall will be the site for the oil tank. (BAE Systems Brough Heritage)*
**Above:** *The tail section of the Shark fuselage, with tailwheel and rudder post fitted. (BAE Systems Brough Heritage)*

*The Shark tail, now with flying surfaces fitted. Note the detachable struts supporting the tailplane. The arrester hook has also been fitted and its design is shown to good effect here. (BAE Systems Brough Heritage)*

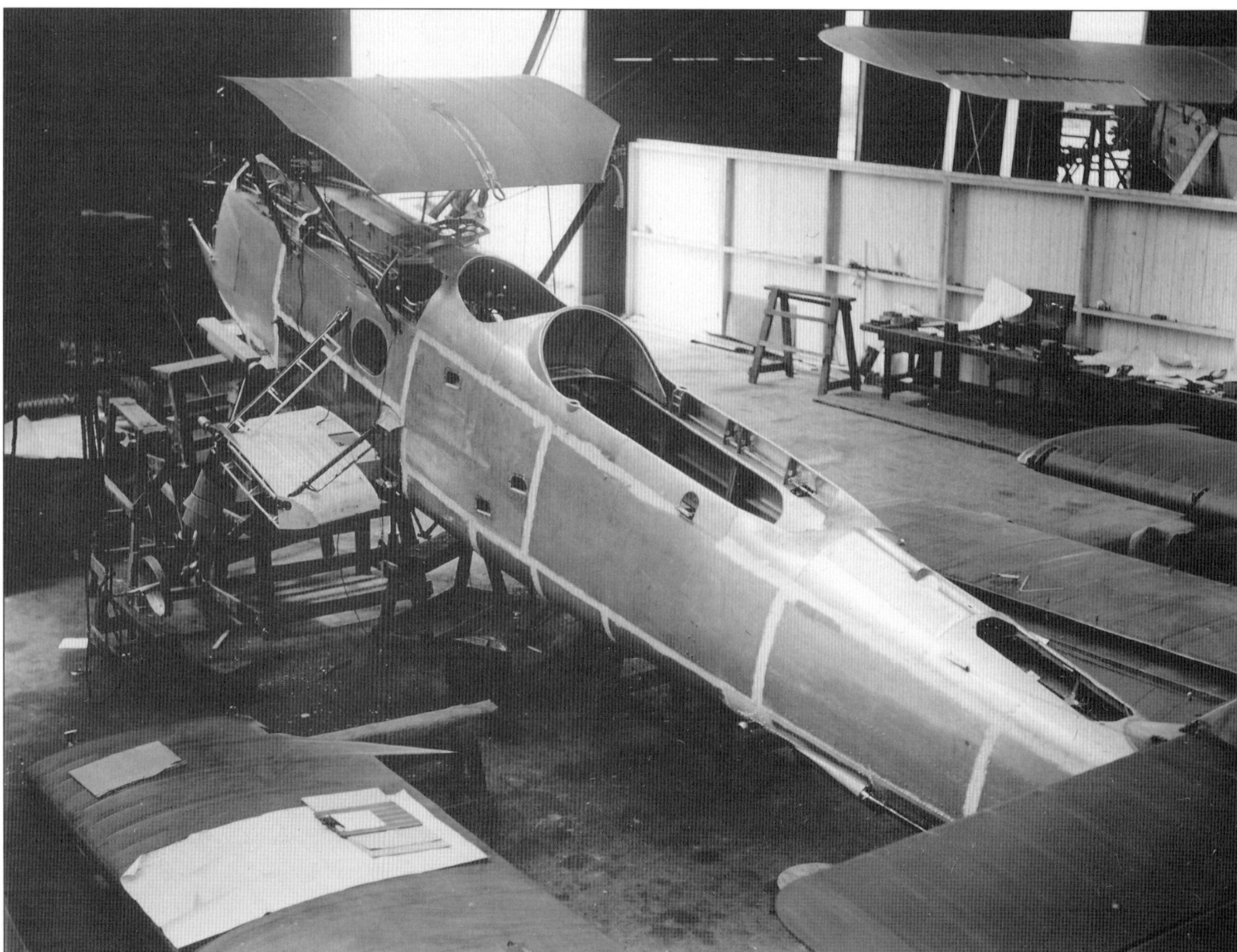

*A Shark airframe at Brough with the flying surfaces partially attached. The cabane has now been assembled, with upper centre-section and lower stub-wings braced by steel-tube struts, and tailplane fitted. The starboard lower wing can be seen beside the fuselage. Flying surfaces are covered in red dope primer. (BAE Systems Brough Heritage)*

*Oil tank installation on an early Shark, mounted just behind the firewall on the port side – the black tube visible at the top left is part of the engine mount. (BAE Systems Brough Heritage)*

*The underside of the prototype K4295, fitted as a floatplane. The torpedo gear, sway-braces and securing cables is apparent. The torpedo carrier was later changed to hold the projectile less nose-down. The oil-cooler, in the upper left of the photograph, was a design not used on any Shark but the prototype. (BAE Systems Brough Heritage)*

*The Robertson oil cooler that was the source of many of the Shark's problems. It was susceptible to the pipes breaking, and it generated a piercing whistle that could be uncomfortable to crews on longer flights. The two exhaust pipes can be seen, with the 'cuffs' that provided hot air to heat the cockpit. (BAE Systems Brough Heritage)*

*The forward fuselage with skin attached and finished, with cabane struts covered in their aerodynamic sheathing. The uncovered section is the trough for the forward-facing machine gun, which also made a useful channel for routing cables and pipes from the engine. (BAE Systems Brough Heritage)*

*The short-chord cowling of the Shark prototype B-6/ K4295 exposed the exhaust collector ring, which can be seen here with various items of ancillary equipment housed inside the engine mount. The exhaust cuffs for cockpit heating are apparent. (BAE Systems Brough Heritage)*

*The Shark's rudder bar and pedals, seen through a removed access panel in the fuselage between the upper and lower cabane struts. (BAE Systems Brough Heritage)*

*The rear cockpit of a production Shark Mk.I, with auxiliary instruments fitted and Lewis gun spare drum stowage visible. Part of the pilot's cockpit, including the top of the spade grip, is also visible. The aircraft in the background is the Segrave II touring monoplane, built by Blackburn to a design by the speed-record holding driver Sir Henry Segrave in 1933-4. (BAE Systems Brough Heritage)*

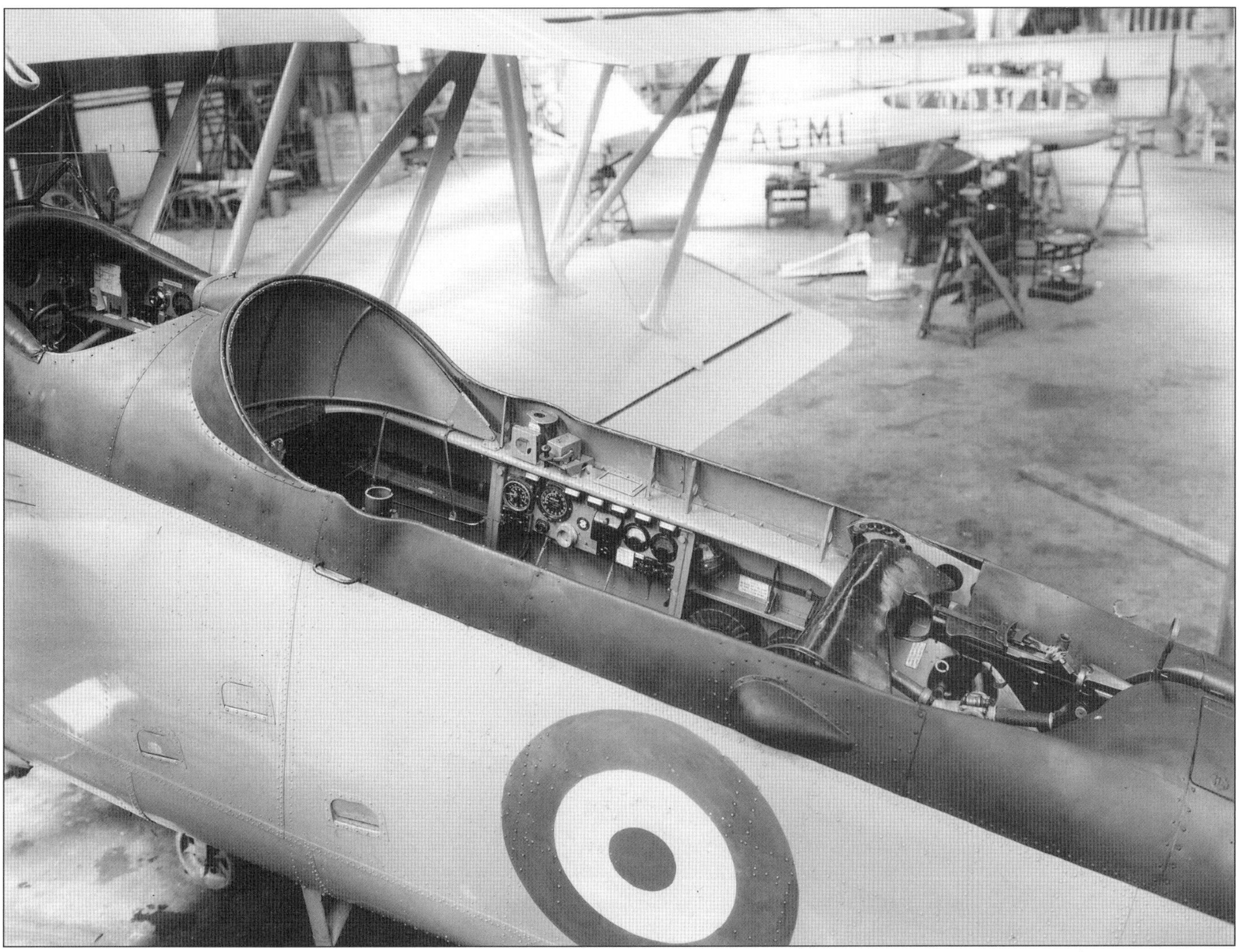

*The rear cockpit of the Shark prototype B-6/K4295, with an airman demonstrating the Lewis gun on its Fairey high speed pillar mounting. The folding cowl at the forward edge of the cockpit to protect the crew from the slipstream is in its raised position. (BAE Systems Brough Heritage)*

*Another view of the B-6 rear cockpit, this time with the Lewis gun stowed, folding cowl retracted and crewmember seated. The triangular fabric panels that would collapse when the upper wings folded can be seen clearly. (BAE Systems Brough Heritage)*

*Another view of the Shark MkI cockpits, showing the folding seat for the Observer. The wire with vertical projections stretched between the forward gunsight and the rear cabane struts is the torpedo sight, used to help judge lay-off on a moving ship. This aircraft is mounted on floats. (BAE Systems Brough Heritage)*

*The pilot's cockpit of the Shark Mk.III from the right, showing the windscreen and sliding canopy, as well as the pilot's seat and the controls on the left hand side. (BAE Systems Brough Heritage)*

*The pilot's cockpit of the Shark Mk.III from the left, showing the control column, pilot's seat and belts. The handle beside the seat is to raise and lower the seat, important with naval aircraft to give the best possible view over the nose for deck-landing. (BAE Systems Brough Heritage)*

*The rear cockpit of the Shark Mk.III, showing the aft part of the sliding canopy, and auxiliary instruments for the Observer/T.A.G., including altitude and airspeed. The gunner's seat is partially visible. (BAE Systems Brough Heritage)*

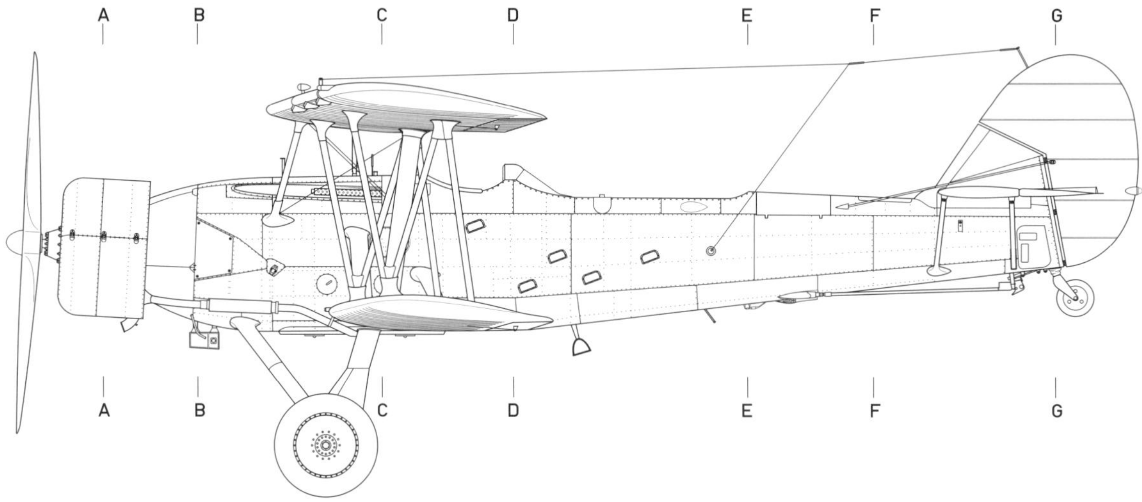


*Blackburn Shark Mk.I (K4352). 1/72 scale.*

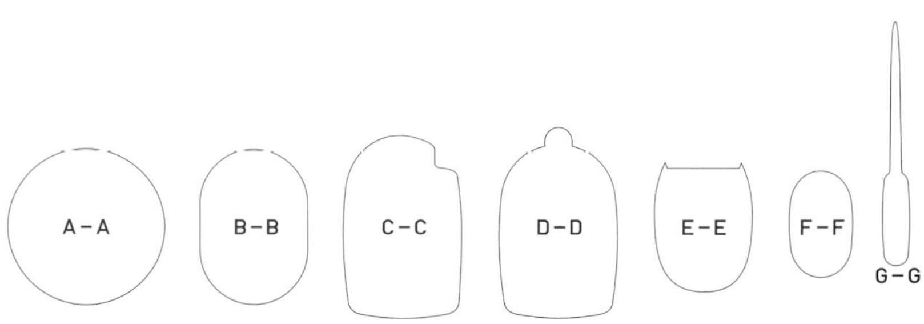

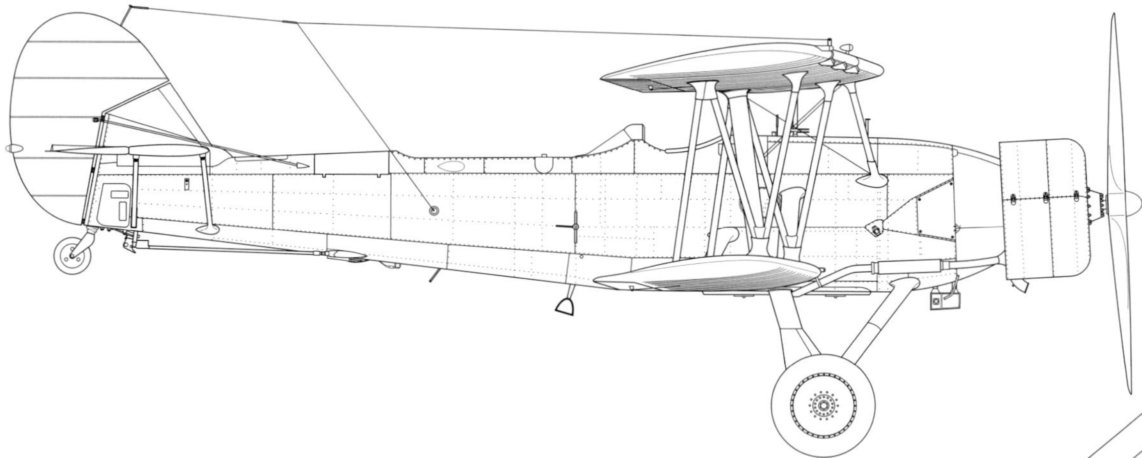

Blackburn Shark Mk.I (K4352). 1/72 scale.

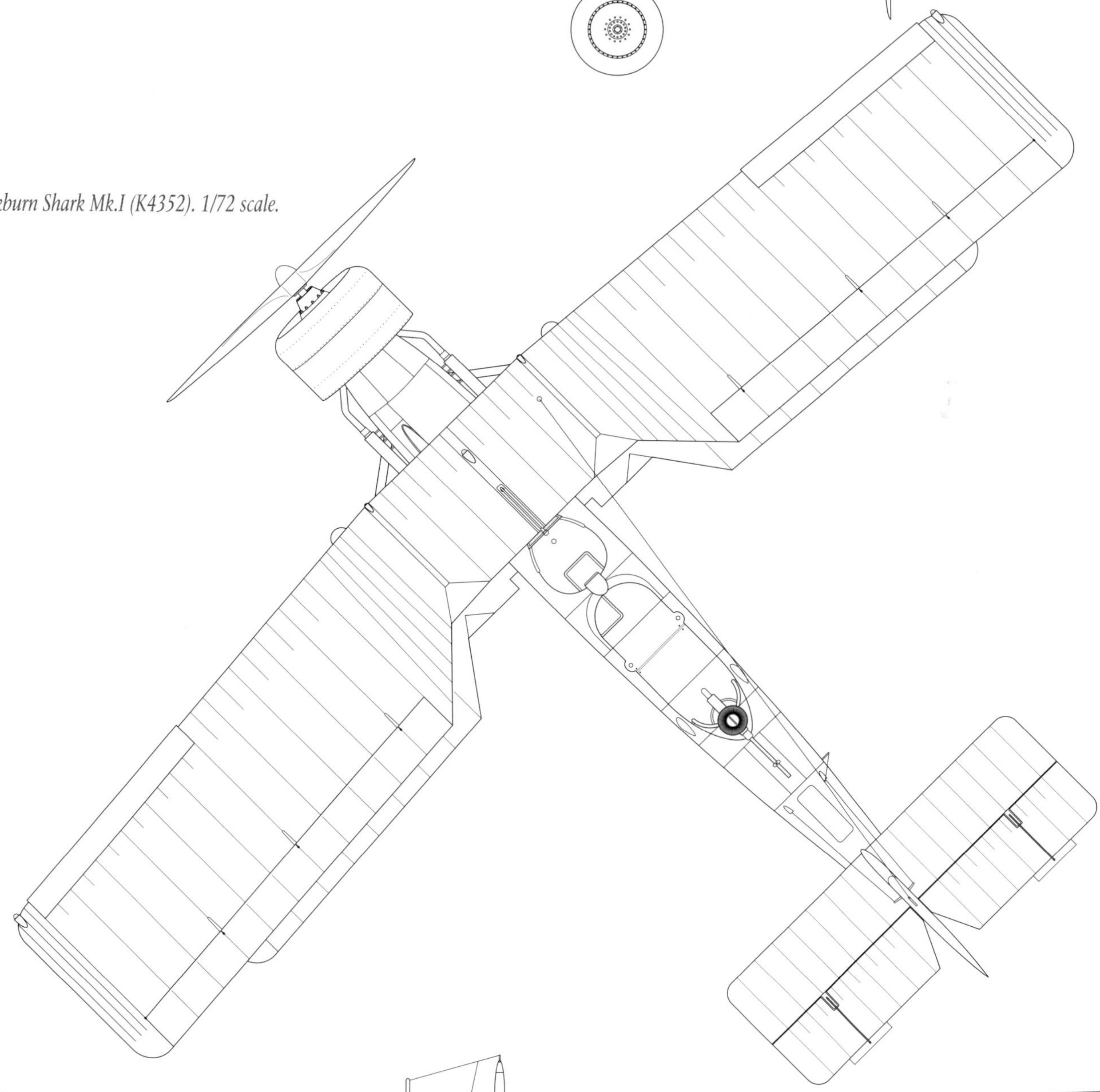

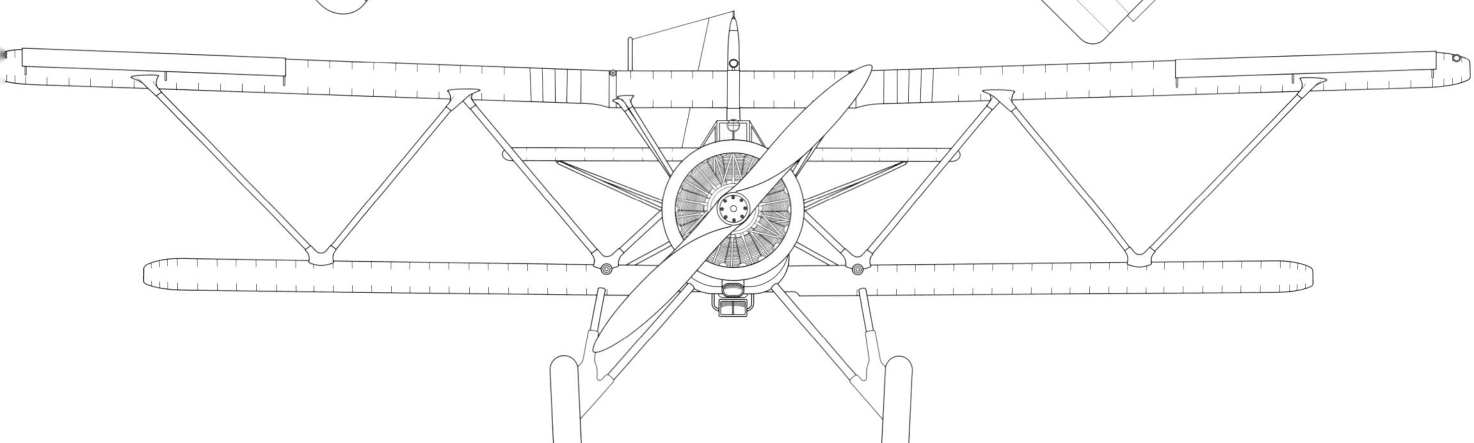

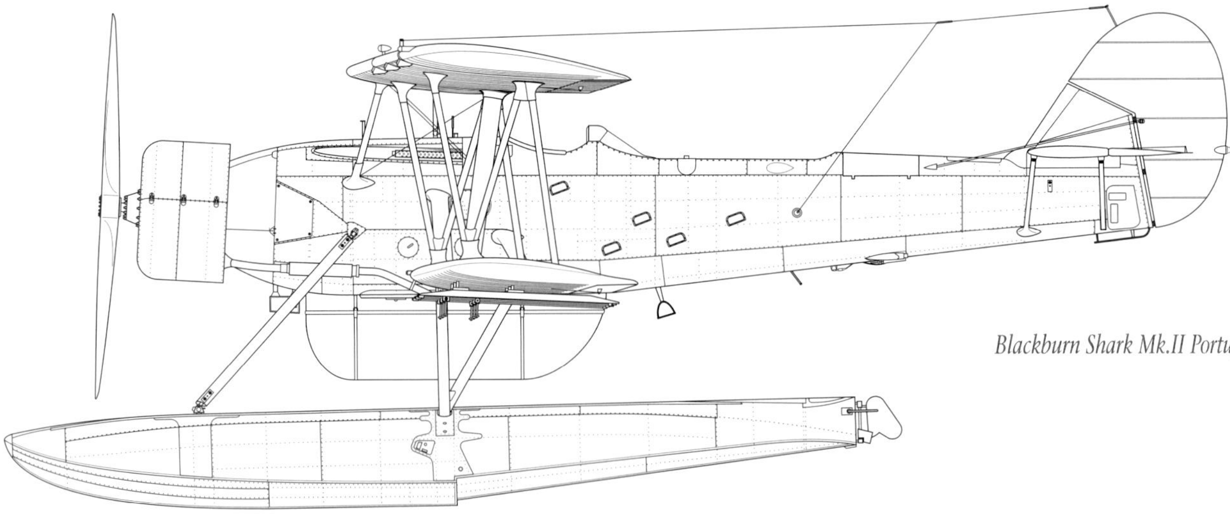

*Blackburn Shark Mk.II Portugal. 1/72 scale.*

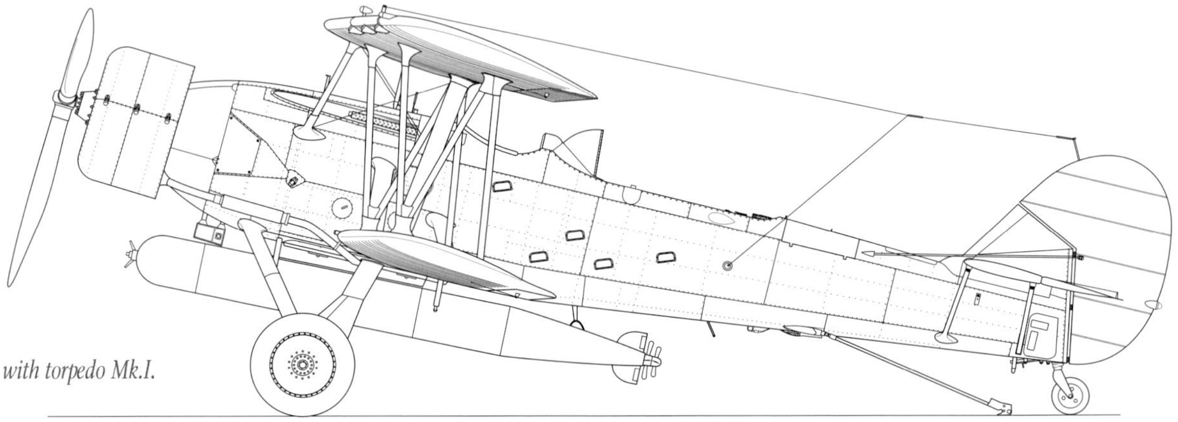

*Blackburn Shark Mk.II with torpedo Mk.I. 1/72 scale.*

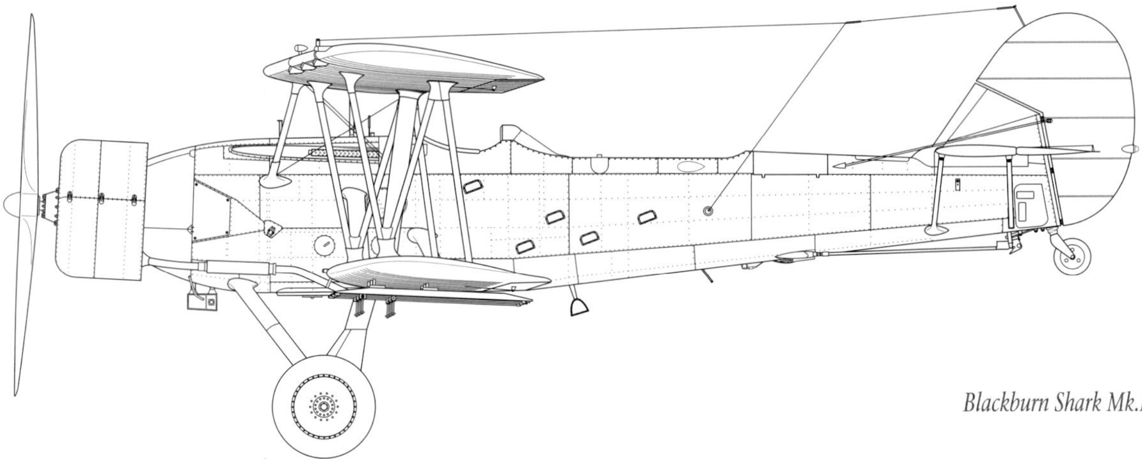

*Blackburn Shark Mk.II (K8490). 1/72 scale.*

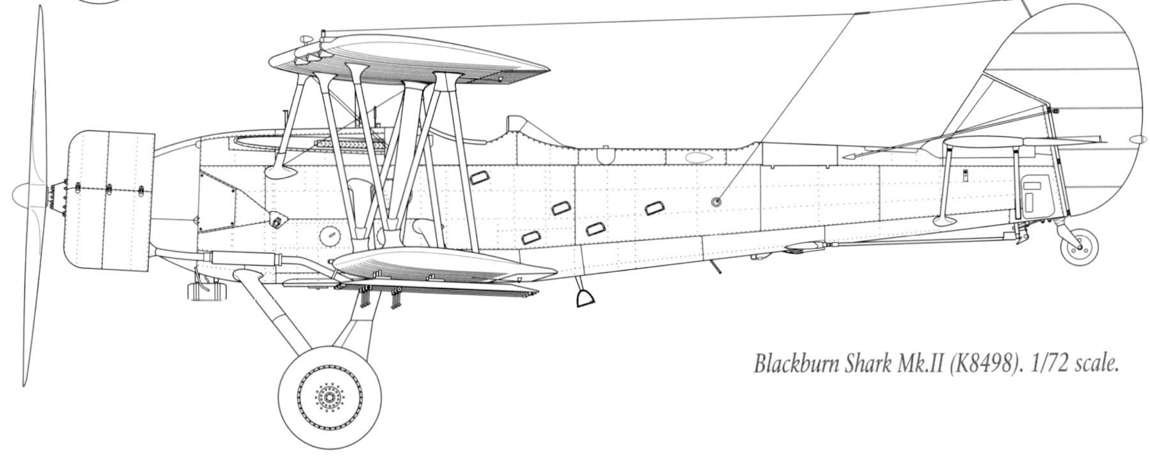

*Blackburn Shark Mk.II (K8498). 1/72 scale.*

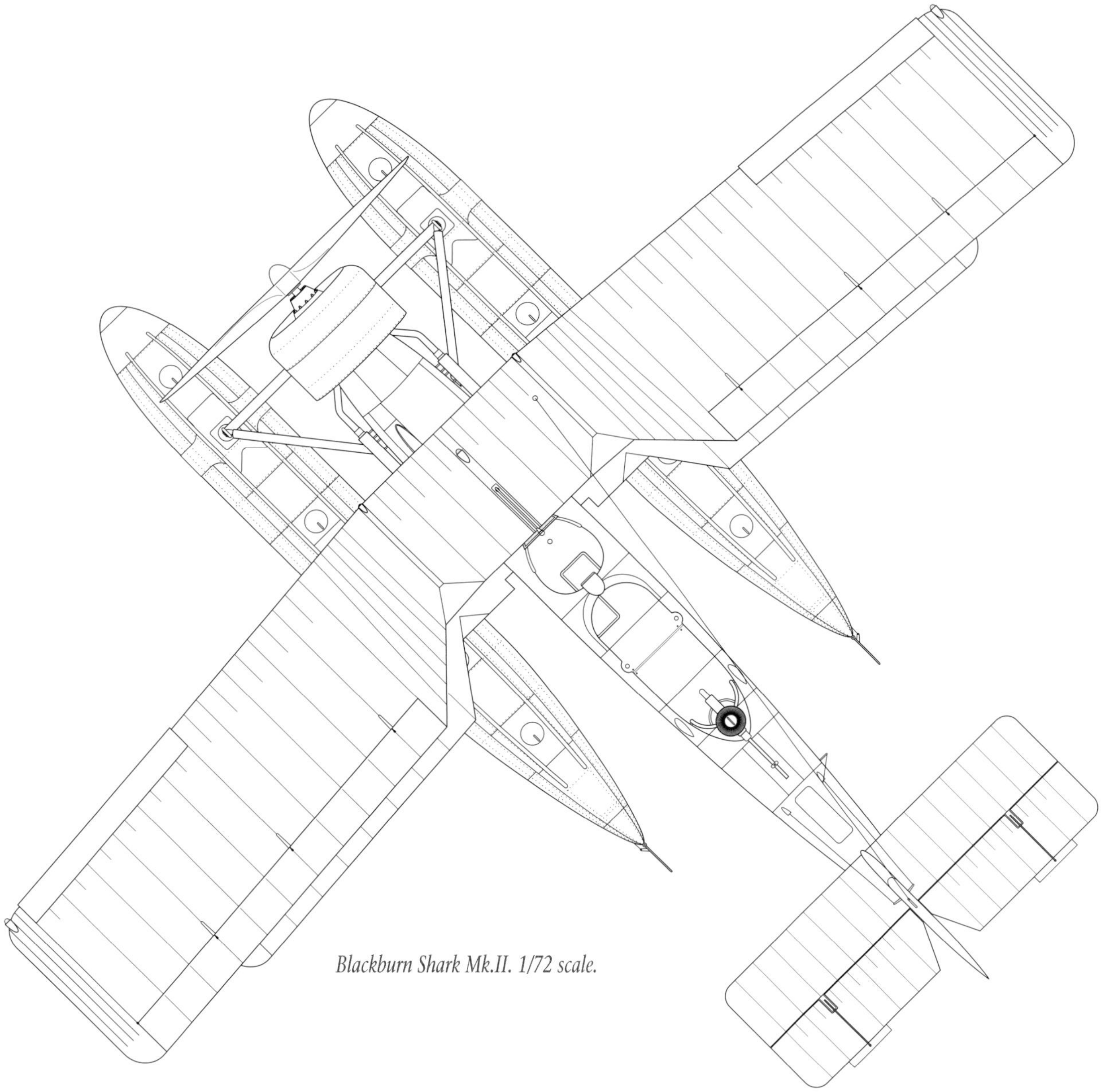

*Blackburn Shark Mk.II. 1/72 scale.*

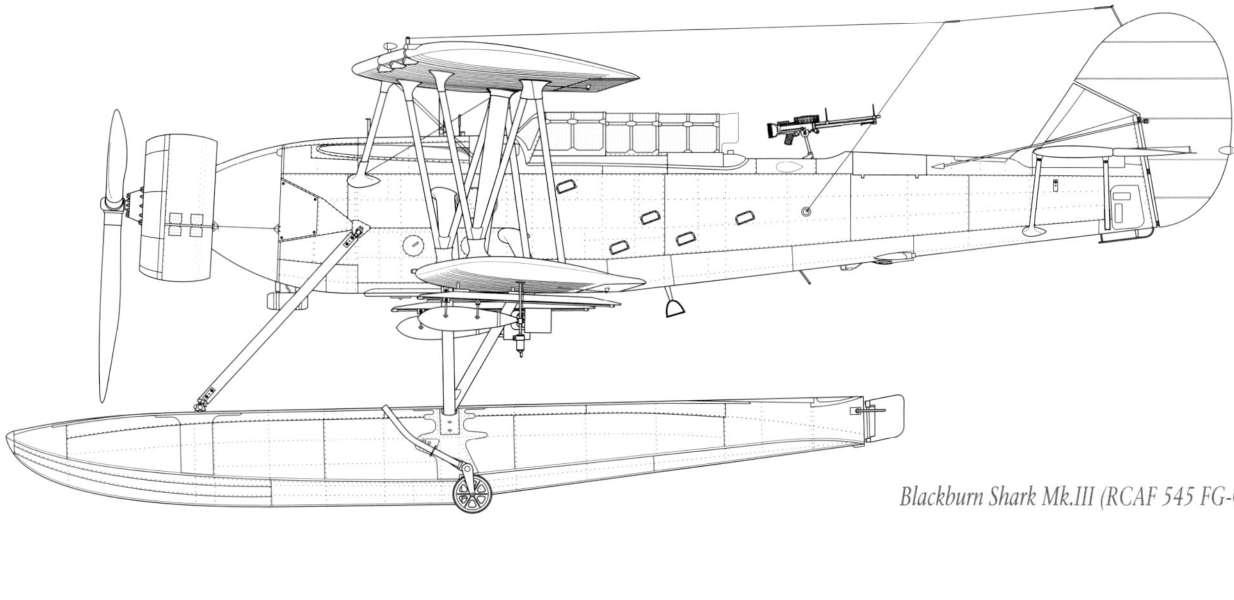

*Blackburn Shark Mk.III (RCAF 545 FG-G). 1/72 scale.*

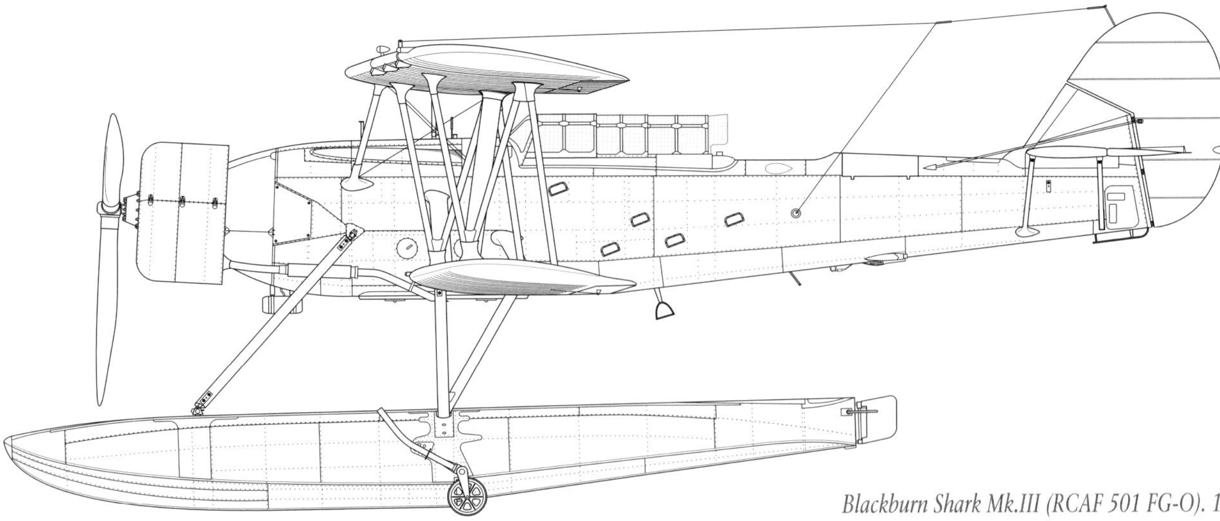

Blackburn Shark Mk.III (RCAF 501 FG-O). 1/72 scale.

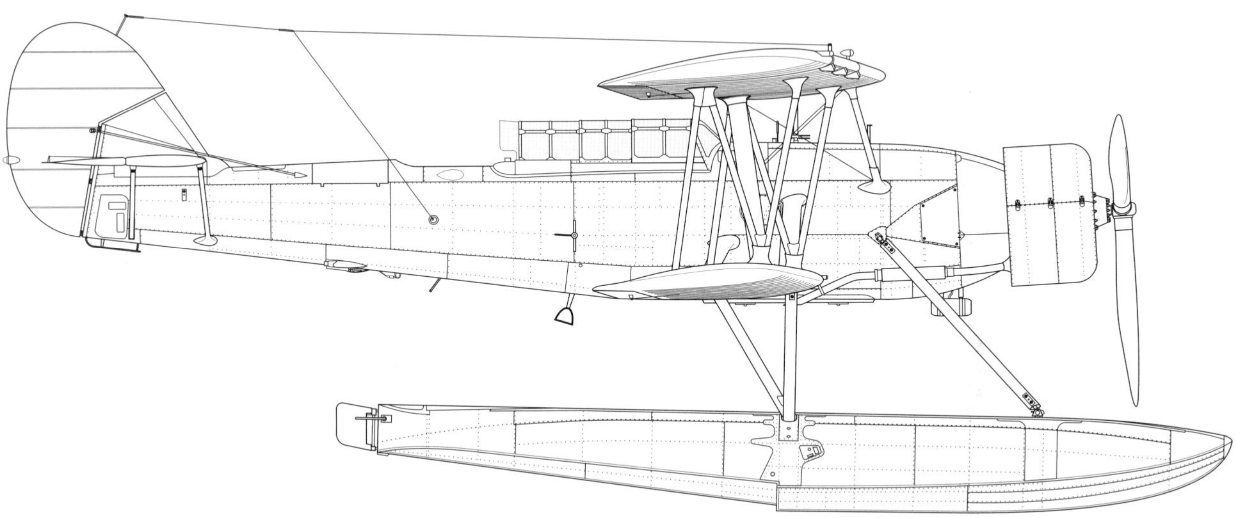

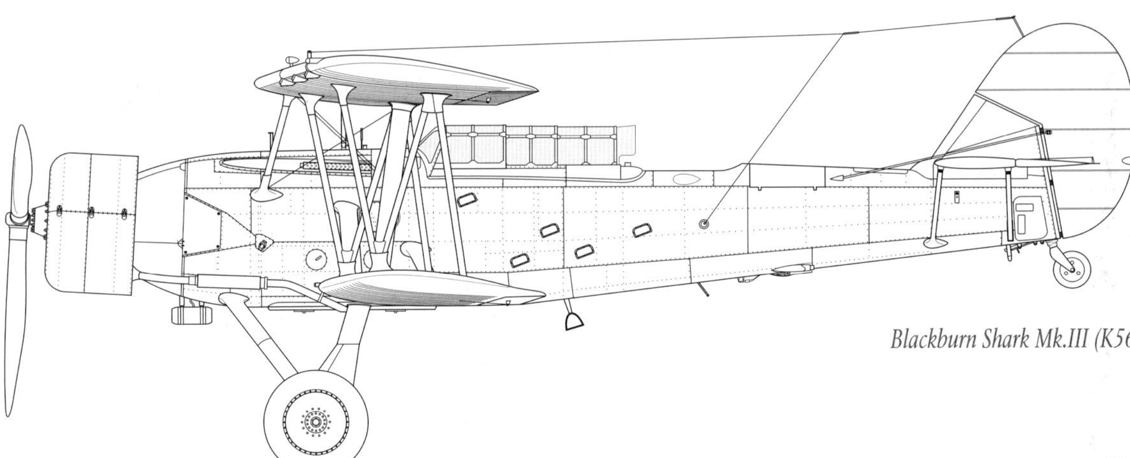

Blackburn Shark Mk.III (K5657). 1/72 scale.

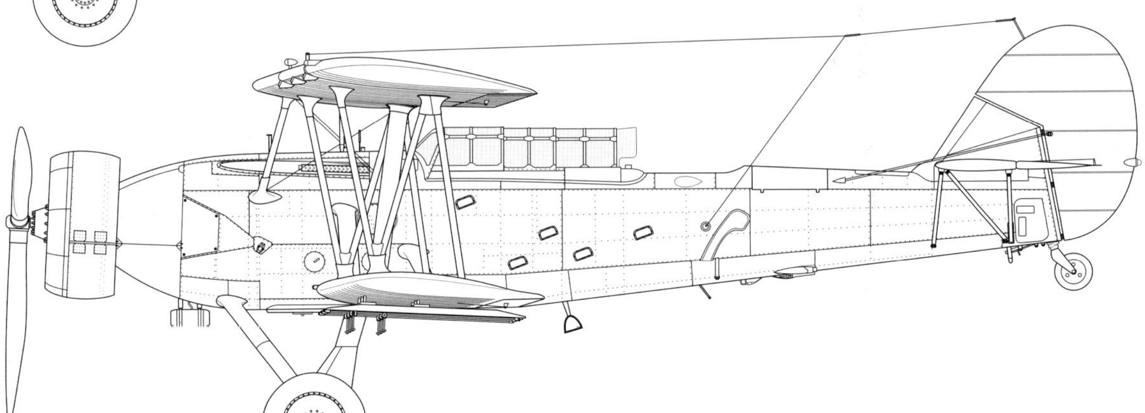

Blackburn Shark Mk.III RCAF. 1/72 scale.

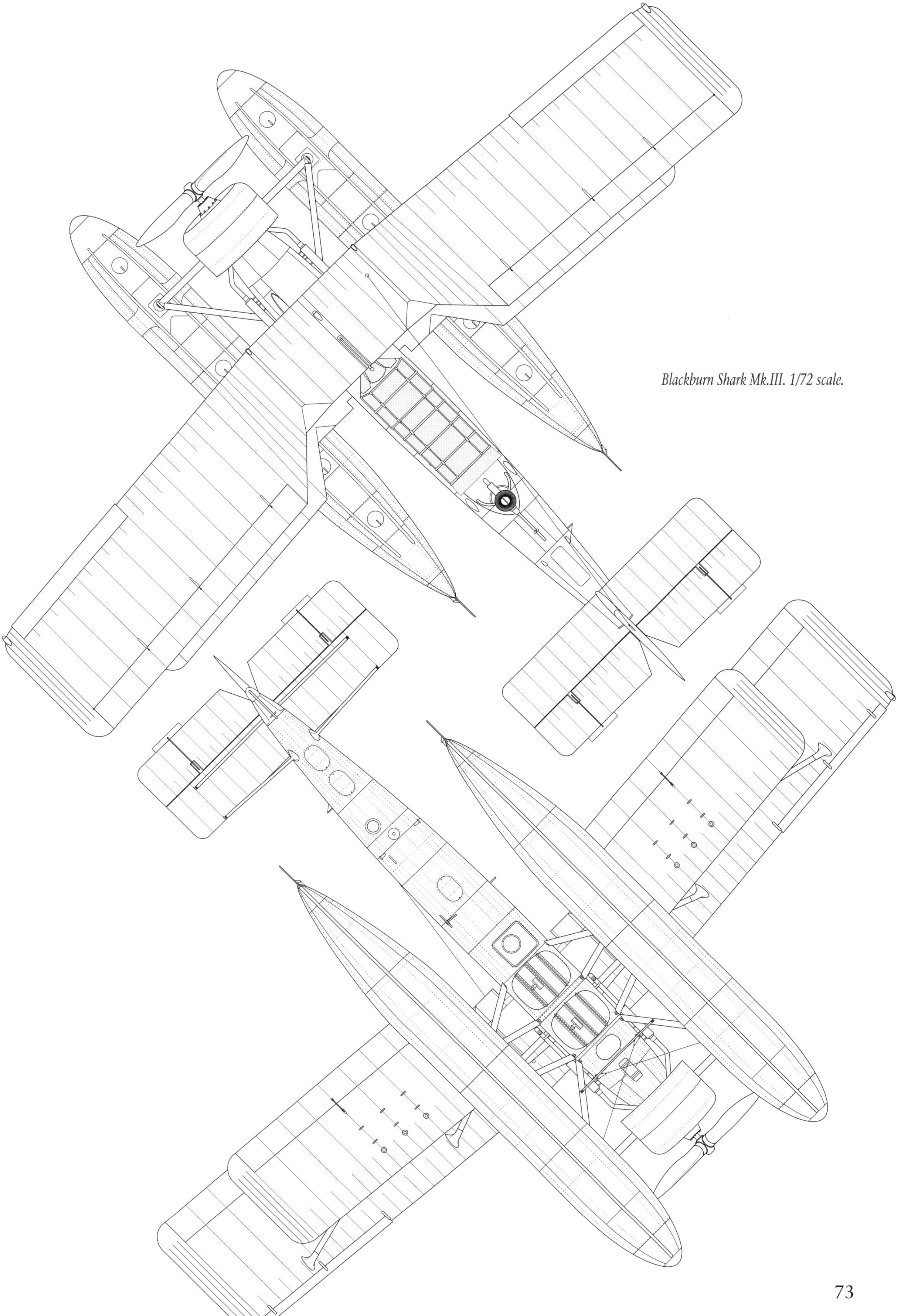

*Blackburn Shark Mk.III. 1/72 scale.*

*Shark Mk.I K4352/740 of 820 Naval Air Squadron in factory finish with squadron markings – the badge on the tail, blue fuselage band (the colour of HMS* Courageous*' air group), with code characters in the early style, and matching coloured wheel discs.*

*Upper view Fleet Air Arm Shark Mk.I/II.*

*Shark Mk.I K4330/647 of 820 Squadron during the unit's time in Egypt in 1936. Note code numbers in a different style to K4352, being larger, thinner and rounder. The squadron emblem is still worn on the fin.*

*Shark Mk.IIA 73-1 of the Portuguese* Aviação Naval, *as delivered 1936.*

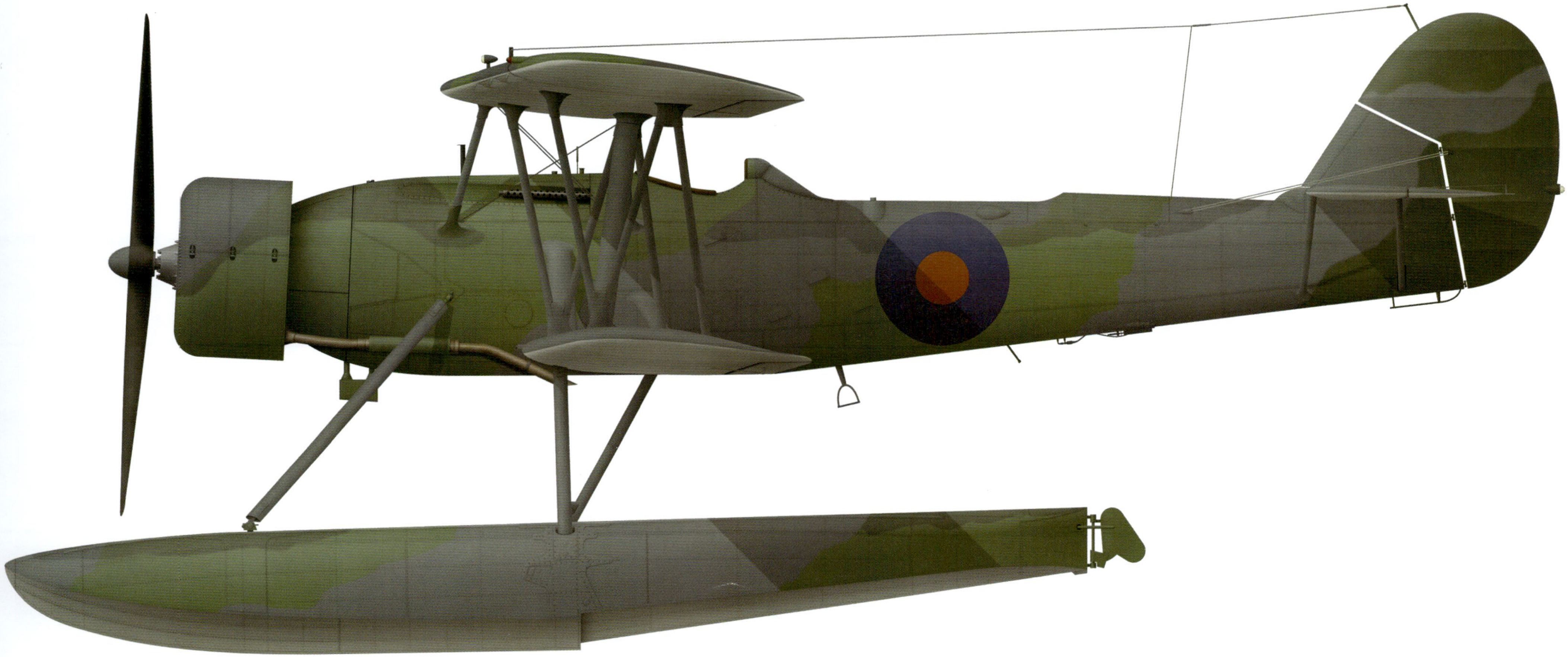

*Shark Mk.II K5616 as it may have looked during camouflage experiments in March 1937, wearing the 'S1C' scheme for temperate conditions. The camouflage incorporated a 'shadow compensating' configuration, with paler colours on lower surfaces – the upper colours were Extra Dark Sea Green and Extra Dark Sea Grey, the lower colours Dark Sea Green and Dark Sea Grey. For more information on these experiments and the schemes worn, see Stuart Lloyd,* Fleet Air Arm Camouflage and Markings: Atlantic and Mediterranean Theatres 1937-41, *Dalrymple & Verdun 2008.*

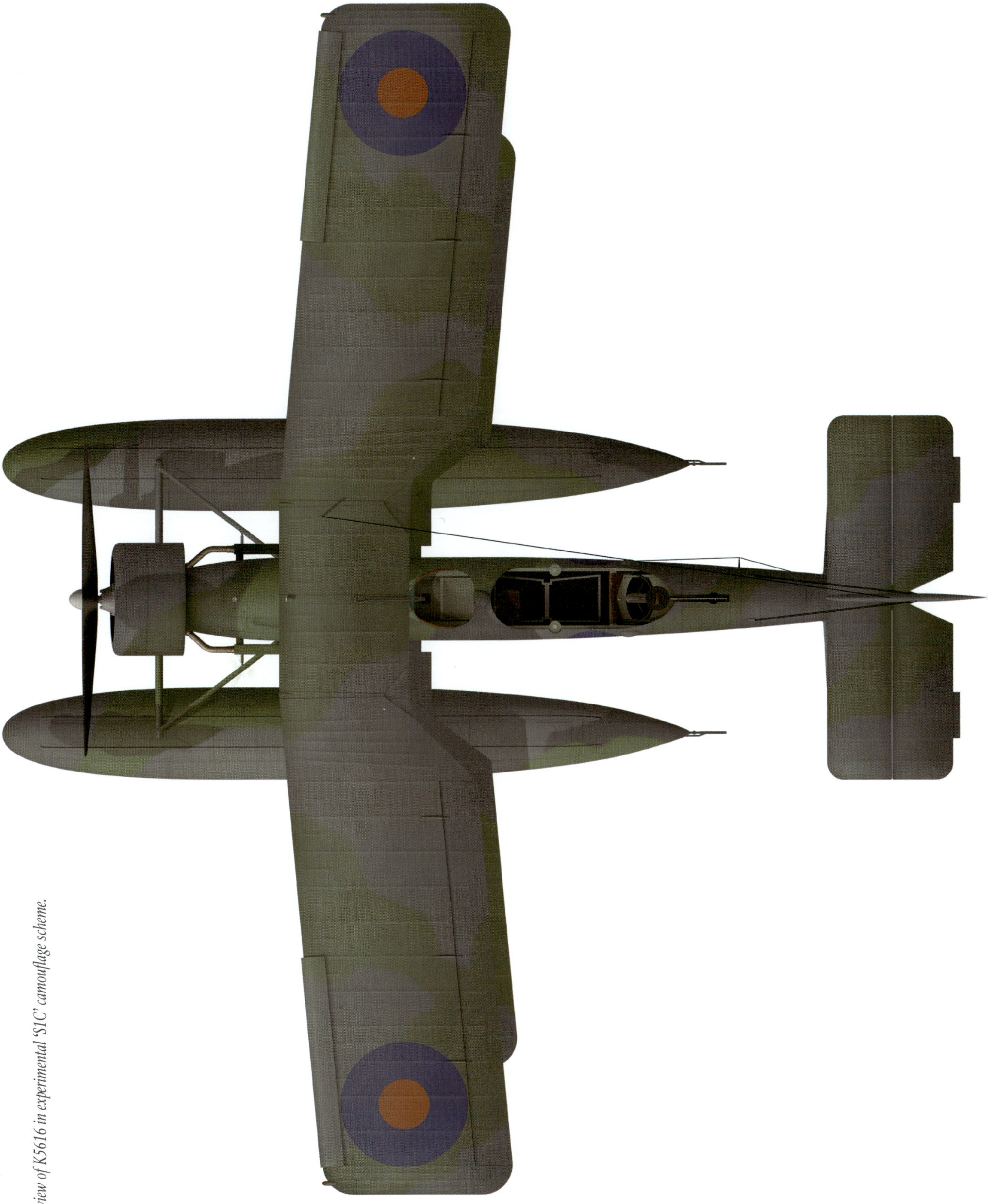

*Upper view of K5616 in experimental 'S1C' camouflage scheme.*

*Shark Mk.IIA Portuguese 74-2 with long range belly tank, as it was seen delivering a dispatch maintaining Portugal's neutrality in the Spanish Civil War in an epic flight from San Jacinto to Calshot in October 1936.*

*Shark Mk.II K5619/682 of 821 Squadron,* HMS Courageous *in 1936-37. This aircraft was lost off Alexandria in February 1937 when it crashed during a navigation exercise. It wears the distinctive style of code numbers typical of this squadron's aircraft.*

*Shark Mk.II K5621/690 of 821 Squadron in 1936, while rigged as a floatplane when the carrier put into Gibraltar. This aircraft wears the same style of thin, square code numbers seen on K5625/680. This Shark was the only one known with certainty to have engaged the enemy, when it bombed a Japanese column in January 1942 during the fighting for Singapore. Ironically it had been withdrawn from frontline use and was in Seletar with 4 Anti-Aircraft Co-operation Unit (A.A.C.U.). It is likely to have been painted in Dark Earth/Dark Green over Sky, though it is impossible to be certain. K5621 is recorded as having worn the code 'R'.*

*Shark Mk.II K5625 rigged as a floatplane, as it served with 444 Flight, as a catapult aircraft for the battle cruiser* HMS Repulse *from May 1936. Aircraft from this 400-series flight do not seem to have worn squadron identifying codes as squadrons did.*

*Shark Mk.II K5625/680 of 821 Squadron aboard HMS Courageous, May 1937. Note the narrow-stroked, square code numbers.*

*Shark Mk.II K5657/902 of 822 Squadron, HMS* Furious*, between November 1936 and March 1937. The style of code numbers was very round in comparison with other squadrons.*

*Shark Mk.II K8436/531 of 810 Squadron,* HMS Courageous, *as it took part in the Coronation Fleet Review for King George VI at Spithead in 1937. The code numbers are rounder and thicker than other squadrons' codes.*

*Shark Mk.II K8466/659 of 820 Squadron aboard HMS* Courageous *in January 1937, at the time it crashed into the carrier's island and was written off in a landing accident while being piloted by Flying Officer Solbe.*

*Shark Mk.II K8485 in around 1941. This aircraft served with various second-line squadrons in the Second World War including 758 Squadron (Eastleigh), 755 Squadron (Worthy Down), 780 Squadron (Lee-on-Solent) and 774 Squadron (St Merryn). By this time it wore the standard scheme for land-based naval aircraft of Temperate Land Scheme camouflage with yellow undersides.*

*Upper view of K8485. Note the 'B' version of the camouflage scheme.*

*Shark Mk.II K8468/654 of 820 Squadron while the squadron was based at Aboukir during fleet manoeuvres in February 1937. Note the code characters, being taller and with thicker strokes, similar to the early style worn on the Mk.I K4352. The wheel disc is the same colour as the fuselage band, with a very light rim, possibly white.*

*Shark Mk.II K8490/537 of 810 Squadron, HMS Courageous 1937, around the time of the Coronation Fleet Review.*

*Shark Mk.II K8498/528 of 810 Squadron aboard HMS* Courageous, *May 1937, when it took part in fleet exercises along with 821 Squadron. Note the newer type of oil-cooler.*

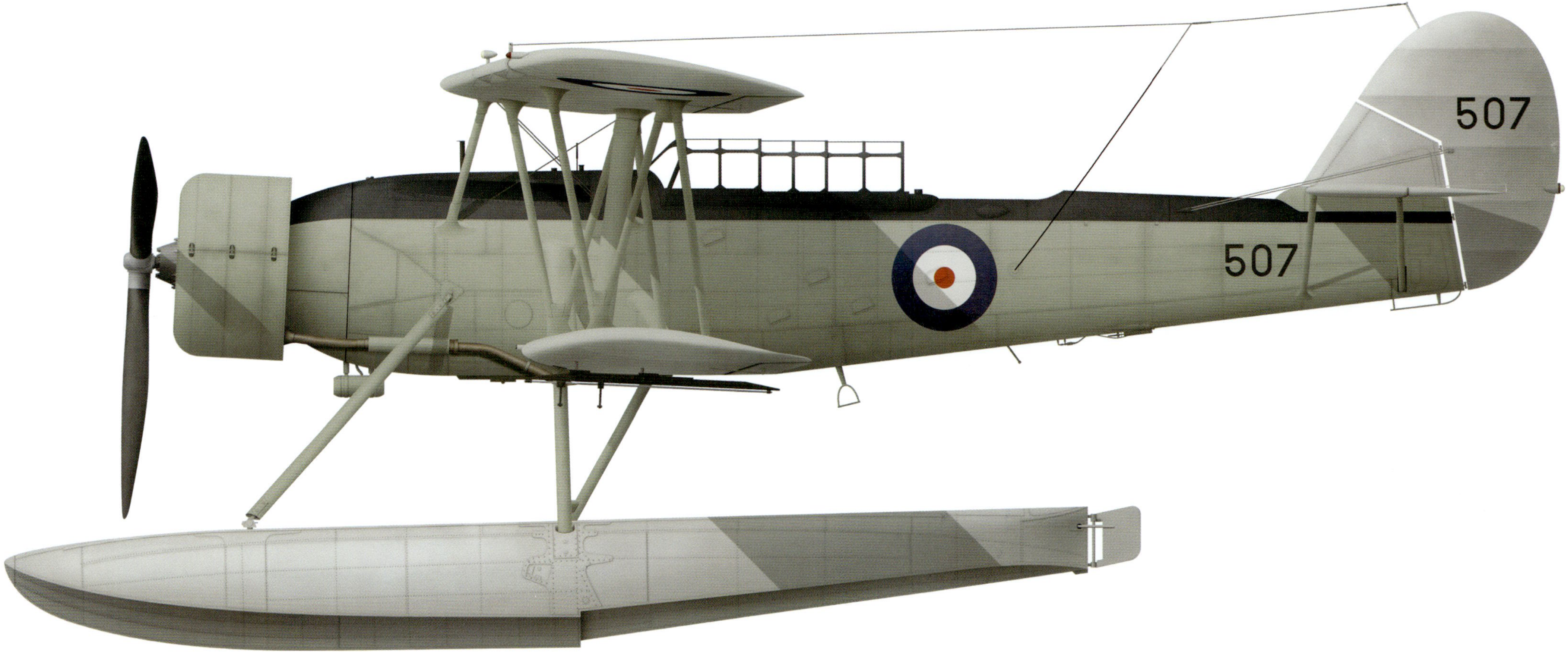


*Shark Mk.II 507 of the Royal Canadian Air Force, of 6 (Torpedo Bomber) Squadron in 1939. As with all British-built RCAF Sharks, it was delivered in the same basic colours as FAA aircraft.*

*Shark K5657 while at the School of Naval Co-operation, RNAS Ford, after its conversion to Mk.III status with an enclosed cockpit and three-blade propeller. The object attached to the fuselage side partially obscuring the roundel is part of the target-towing installation.*

*Shark Mk.III K8891/W4P of 753 Squadron, Lee-on-Solent in July 1940. The colour scheme here is slightly speculative based on available evidence, but photographs showing a low-contrast camouflage scheme and contemporary documentary information suggest that at this time the aircraft wore a modified S1E 'Sea Scheme' of Extra Dark Sea Grey/Dark Slate Grey camouflage over Sky Grey. Being a land-based aircraft, the Shark should have worn a land scheme, but confusion abounded in wartime naval aircraft colours during this period and aircraft were frequently painted in incorrect schemes. Instructions stated that TBR aircraft, which Sharks had been even though now only used for training, should be painted in the scheme. This, and the fact that 753 Squadron was a naval unit, may account for the discrepancy.*

*Shark Mk.III K8911 of 750 Squadron Observers' school at RNAS Ford in 1939. The reason for the stripe along the fuselage, which was probably red, is unknown.*

*Shark Mk.III L2361/W1W at 750 Squadron school for Observers in early 1939. Identifying markings include a black cowling front and mainwheel disc, and the unusually placed small code 'W1W' on the fin.*

*Shark Mk.III L2369 at the School of Naval Co-operation, Lee-on-Solent and Ford, 1937-8.*

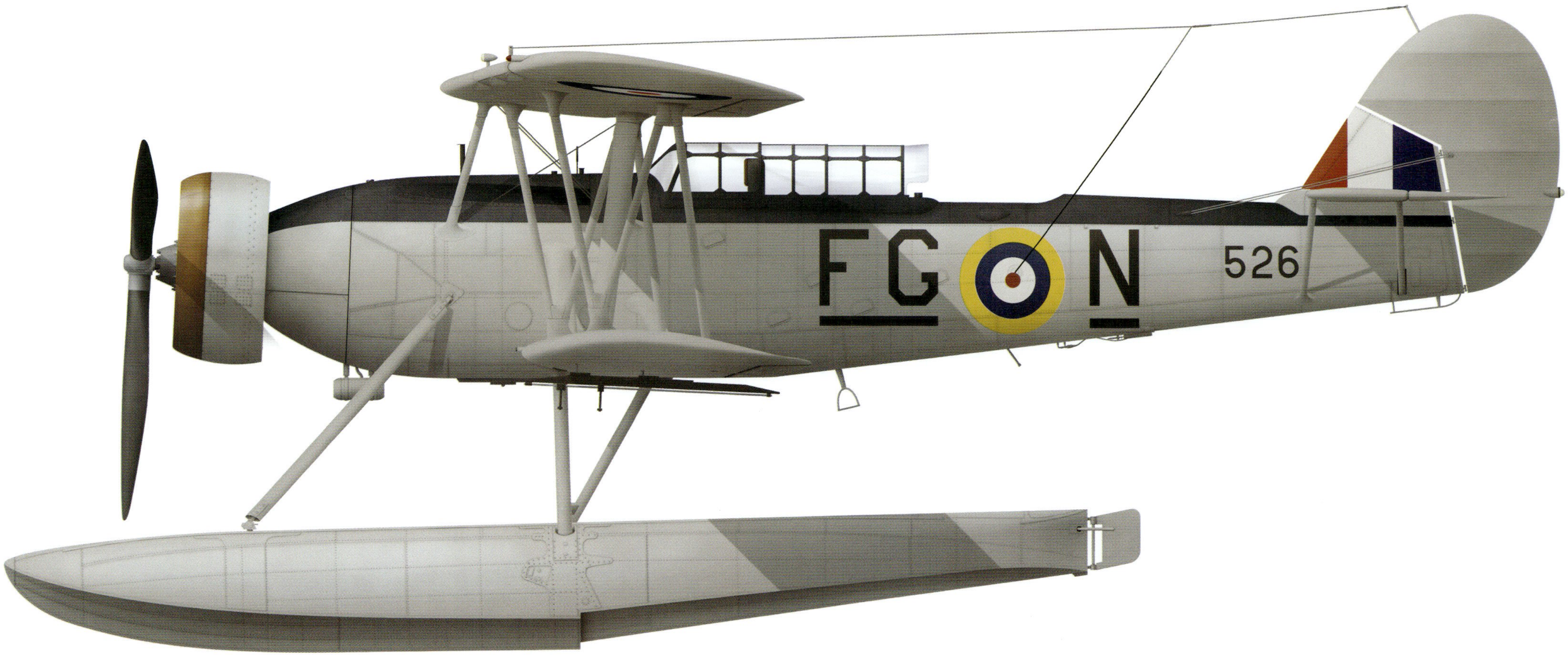


*Shark Mk.III 526/FG-N – the last Blackburn-built Shark – of 7 (BR) Squadron, Prince Rupert, September 1942. The red-white-blue-yellow roundels were worn on the fuselage at that time. The colour scheme at this time was the same as Canadian-built Sharks, being all-over dull aluminium apart from the black upper fuselage deck. The aircraft carried the serial number in thin black characters under the lower wings.*

*Shark Mk.II 501/FG-O of 7 (Bomber Reconnaissance) Squadron RCAF in Summer 1942, at Prince Rupert, British Columbia, having been repainted in all-over grey at some point since 1940, replacing the initial factory scheme.*

*Shark Mk.III (Canadian) 524/XE-M of 6 (Bomber Reconnaissance) Squadron in 1940 at Alliford Bay in the Queen Charlotte Islands. Aircraft of 6 Squadron wore reduced-visibility red-blue roundels on the fuselage at this time, retaining the red-white-blue roundels above and below the upper wing.*

*Shark Mk.II 504/AG-D with 122 (Composite) Squadron, Patricia Bay, British Columbia, in 1942, wearing its distinctive and unusual black and yellow target tug markings. Unlike RAF and FAA target tug schemes, RCAF Shark target tug stripes were symmetrical across the aircraft, and the black stripes more widely placed. Shark 504 wore a red-blue roundel above the upper wing, and red-white-blue roundel in other locations*

*Upper view of 504/AG-D, demonstrating the 'mirror image' stripes.*

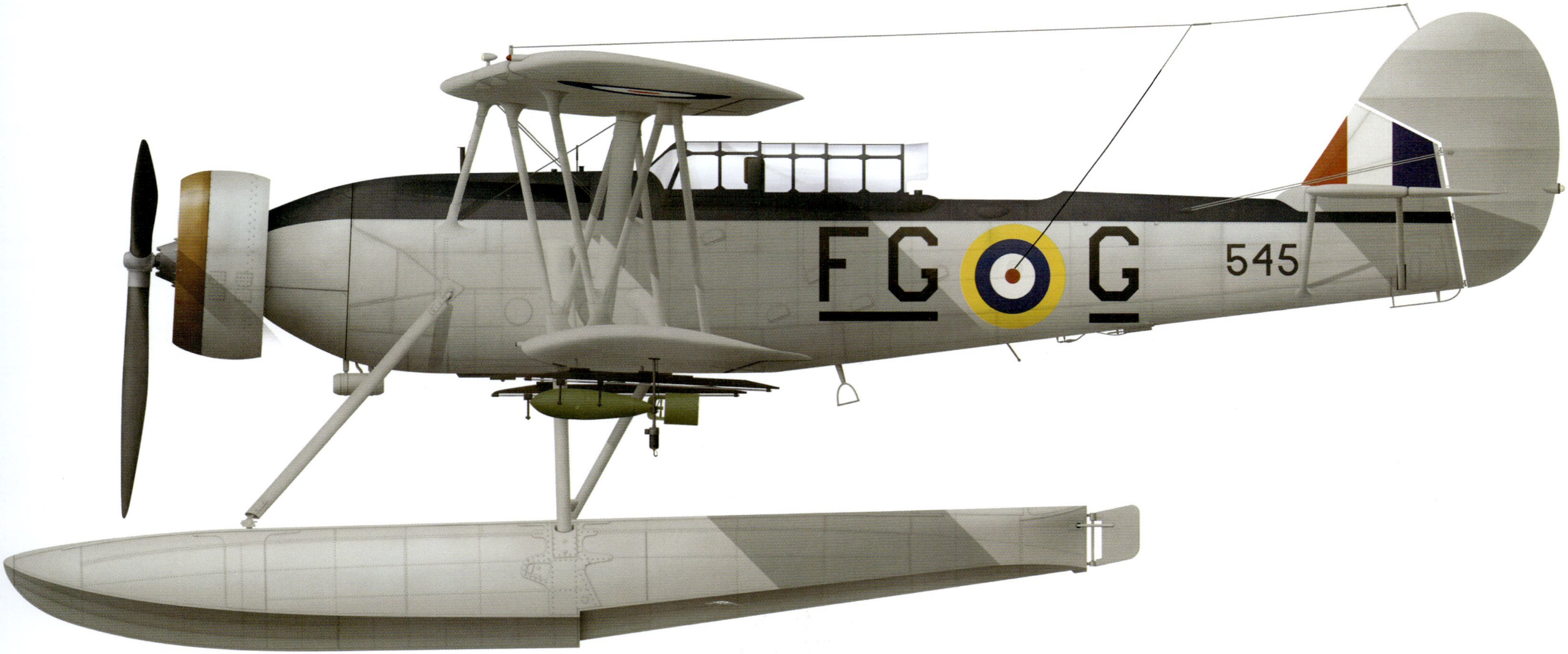


*Shark Mk.III (Canadian) 545/FG-G of 7 (BR) Squadron RCAF at Prince Rupert in 1942. This aircraft was built by Boeing, and its colour scheme was typical of Canadian-built Sharks. It wore its serial beneath the lower wing and red-white-blue roundel above and below the upper wing.*